email ...@yahoo.co.uk
Tel: 07878 760 609   £12

OUR CHILDREN ARE SPIRITS

I hope fathers will forgive me but this book is dedicated to mothers, for obvious reasons. Not less obvious is my decision to dedicate it especially to Inez, who will receive this testimonial of love and affection on behalf of all of you. Without her it would have been impossible to accomplish the endeavor of successfully bringing three spirits from the invisible dimension into our lives as our children so that they would be able to share the privilege of life with us.

Translated by
Mary Ann Harvey Magalhães
Maria Júlia Porchat- Secco

Revised by
Marco Antonio Penteado

The original portuguese title *Nossos filhos são espiritos*, published by "Editora 3 de outubro", 11th edition, june 2010, Bragança Paulista, SP, Brasil,
e-mail : editoratresdeoutubro@gmail.com

ALL RIGHTS RESERVED. This book contains material protected under International and Federal Copyright Laws and Treaties. Any unauthorized reprint or use of this material is prohibited. No part of this book may be reproduced or transmitted in any form or by any means, electronic or mechanical, including photocopying, recording, or by any information storage and retrieval system without express written permission from the author / publisher.

Editions SF / Librairie Spirite Francophone.
Internet Access : http://www.editions-sf.com/
Email : info@editions-sf.com

© 2010, Librairie Spirite Francophone
ISBN : 1453823093
EAN : 9781453823095

CONTENTS

INTRODUCTION..7
THE STORY BEHIND AN UNEXPECTED BOOK...................................9
Chapter 1. EYES THAT SEE AND EYES THAT LOOK..........................11
Chapter 2. THINGS WE MUST UNLEARN..14
Chapter 3. HOW TO REORDER YOUR THOUGHTS............................18
Chapter 4. RESPONSIBILITY..20
Chapter 5. A FLASK OF POISON..25
Chapter 6. TODY OR MANY HALLEYS FROM NOW?........................31
Chapter 7. BEING BORN IS THE PROBLEM, NOT DYING 34
Chapter 8. WHAT ARE WE BORN FOR?..38
Chapter 9. REFLEXIONS ON ADOPTION..42
Chapter 10. WELL, LET'S GO!..48
Chapter 11. MYSTERIES OF THE COMMUNICATION PROCESS........52
Chapter 12. UNDERSTANDING THROUGH TALKING........................57
Chapter 13. A YOUNG MOTHER'S EXPERIENCE AND
OBSERVATIONS...62
Chapter 14. WE ONLY FORGET WHAT WE KNOW.............................68
Chapter 15. PEOPLE WHO CAN REMEMBER PAST LIVES.................74
Chapter 16. BEING A MEDIUM IS NOT A TRAGEDY..........................84
Chapter 17. DOM BIAL AND HIS FRIEND BLATFORT........................90
Chapter 18. THE MUCH DISCUSSED INFLUENCE OF THE
ENVIRONMENT..101
Chapter 19. HANDICAPPED CHILDREN..107
Chapter 20. THE DRAMATIC WORDS OF A SPIRIT...........................115
Chapter 21. THE GIRL CRYING ON THE SIDEWALK........................120
Chapter 22. THERE IS NO NEED TO
"BEND IT WHILE STILL A TWIG"...125
Chapter 23. THE PRESENCE OF GOD..131
Chapter 24. HOW TO TALK TO GOD..139
Chapter 25. THE PS THAT BECAME A CHAPTER..............................146
Chapter 26. FROM THE SOLID STATE TO THE GAS STATE.............152
Chapter 27. "SEE YOU"...158
Chapter 28. THE JOB CALLED LIFE...163
Chapter 29. "FATHER DIPLOMA"...167
Chapter 30. MY FATHER DIPLOMA PART 2: THE MISSION.............171
BIBLIOGRAPHY...200

INTRODUCTION

It is now over 30 years since we follow what Herminio Miranda has been writing. We place him among the best spiritist writers. This gives him, based on his qualified work, a natural space that will have a reflection not only in our days, but also in the days to come and much after.

In these unpretencious lines, as an introduction, we wish to present to the readers, with no intention of personal praise, a valuable book, dotted with well elaborated and suggestive remarks in face of daily happenings, where the author emphasizes facts of childhood and past memories.

Herminio's book is eloquent, as it touches the social side of life and is more than useful as it searches for explanations for our own reason for living. His words positively call for the reconstrution of faith, aiming its purest concepts. Some religious movements that should enhance religion, have taken it to almost total ruin.

The purpose of this book is deeper than the ideas themselves. Its well placed descriptions will allow the reader to reach the horizons of psychological boundaries. The simple and clarifying concepts are a suitable call for the perfection of our earthly needs.

The author writes for the reader's benefit. It is a talent that belongs to him, conquered through his many lives. His thoughts are placed in harmonious propositions, reviving ethics in face of nowaday's social and even religious failures. The child personality has been translated in its spiritual principles, allowing to a more precise view of human purposes.

All over the book one can feel a captivating, constructive and always renewing breath, inviting us to knowlege and better still, calls our attention to the responsibilities contained in the infinite road to evolution. The lively stories take us to understading – in the depth of psychological reasons- the roots of inconsciousness or spirit, with its telegraphic suggestions to the physical intelect - the conscious zone or personality.

The main value of the author lies in his constant search for a goal- the knowlegde of the spiritual facts that are present in our every day life and of which many people still dont realize the existence and are actually unaware of its presence. However, they are important links in the path of our lives.

The contents of this work has a rich sequency of well organized ideas, all with a purpose. If we carefully observe the chapters in the book, we will notice that although each one has its distinct and unmistakable subject, they together belong to a chain that can be translated in an authentic saga. The good scribbler succeeded in turning short stories into beautiful and harmonious songs; and because they talk to our souls, they turned out into a symphony.

Jorge Andrea dos Santos
Rio de Janeiro, January 24, 1989

THE STORY BEHIND AN UNEXPECTED BOOK

There is always a story behind a book, a person, an animal, a country, a city and a civilization. It might not even be an exciting story, an adventure like the history of the Hebrews, but there is always something to tell. This book, for example, came about unexpectedly. It was never in my plans. One day a close friend of mine asked me out of the blue: "Why don't you write a book about children?"

I was very surprised at the suggestion and said nothing. "A book about children?" "I don't know the first thing about children." I thought. Later I realized that it wasn't such a crazy idea after all; maybe I could do it. At that point my mind was already working in silence. When I started writing it seemed the book was ready in some mysterious drawer of my mind. Slowly things started coming out and I began putting them down on paper. In a little over a month it was ready.

And then there was another surprise: the readers loved it! When the fourth edition was due I thought it was time to update it. I thought I should add some information and feedback and give it new "clothing". I wanted especially to thank the thousands of readers who chose to read what I had to say about children. It seems they liked it. At least this is what they tell me in person, by letter or telephone. And, naturally, it was very good to know that so many people enjoyed what I had written. Thank you and God bless you all.

HCM
Autumn, 1993

Chapter 1.
EYES THAT SEE AND EYES THAT LOOK

Dr. Pimentel cut the umbilical cord, wrapped the baby in a cloth – it was a girl – laid her carefully on her stomach and turned to care for the mother who was exhausted and in pain.

I was 23 and for the first time in my life I was overwhelmed by the powerful emotions of fatherhood with all its perplexities, complexities and expectations. I walked over to the little bundle of joy that was my daughter and looked at her very closely for the first time. I thought she would be asleep still dreaming of where she had come from. I was surprised to see that she was wide awake, and her bright dark eyes looked at me in a curious and enigmatic way. I can still remember the wrinkles on her small forehead from the effort she was making to lift up her tiny bald head, as if she was asking herself: "Will he be a good father to me?" "Where is my mother?" "What are they going to do to me now?" "How long am I going to be here, wrapped in this cloth?"

As far as I am concerned I do not recall the thoughts that crossed my mind but I know they were many and disconnected. I believe I had as many questions as she did, maybe even more, I don't know.

But I was sure of one thing: Ana Maria had just arrived (I knew her name because we had already chosen it beforehand and although there was a boy's name in store, in some way I knew it would be a girl). Mysteries as these I understand better today than at that time.

There was no doubt, however, that she had arrived; for there she was, with her questioning eyes eager to start exploring the new world she had come to live in. I had different doubts. I kept asking myself "where did she come from? Logic would tell me that if she had arrived here it was because she had left from some place where she had been before, but where then?

A long time ago, as a child, I had learned that God created a brand-new soul for each new-born but I had always found it hard to

CHAPTER 1.

accept this idea, as well as many others. There was no doubt in my mind about the power, the greatness and the wisdom of God that was so clear in front of me in that very tiny person which we, my young wife and I, could obviously not have made out of nothing.

Later, I would learn that human beings discover things but do not create or invent them and we had certainly not created that little warm bundle, a true human being who looked at me with so much attention.

Who was that small being? Where did she come from? What would be her purpose in life? What would she be like in the future? What role would her mother and I have in this life that had just started? Or would it be that it had not just started but was continuing?

I would not know. But I very much wanted to have answers for these and other questions which I hardly remember or have not even been formulated before, because, as I said, I had plunged into a whirlpool of unexpected and unsuspected emotions. These emotions, however, didn't make me fearful or doubtful but brought me a strange happiness as I noticed that I also had the possibility of participating with my humble contribution in that wonderful spectacle of renovation of life.

These doubts were left for later on. One day I would know, I must have thought. Meanwhile there were things to do on this side of life where beings have arrived a long time ago and where they walk, talk, laugh and cry. But it would surely be nice to have someone there to tell me what was going on before me.

So this is the book I would like to have had in my hands not only on that distant August 22 but before when Ana Maria was only a project, well before her personal clock started clicking here on Earth.

Some of my questions would still have to wait for quite some years. Others, I believe, will need some more centuries as our Almighty Father does not seem to be in a hurry to clarify things we are still unable to grasp.

Paul, the apostle who was so wise, writes to the Corinthians (1 Corinthians 3:16) "And I, brethren, could not speak unto you as unto spiritual, but as unto carnal, [even] as unto babes in Christ.; I have fed you with milk, and not with meat: for hitherto ye were not able to bear it, neither yet now are you able, because you still live as people of this world do."

Like the Corinthians I was living in the flesh and I think I hadn't been given any milk, because all I could see was that, in some way, there was a little bit of me in that tiny being who was waiting to be picked up in our arms and, later on, hand in hand with us, shown what our world was like. On that day looking ahead into the future I could foresee the day she would no longer need our hands and would leave to live her own life.

We are somehow always a little fearful. It is not lack of trust, but somehow there is always a slight fear that the baby bird will not find the invisible path it will have to go through in its still unsure flight. But it was not sadness because, after all, it was her life and not ours and, as I would later learn, before being children of one another we are all children of one only Father. And He has been very competent in looking after us.

It was not sadness, not at all! But a slight longing, that peered at me from the folds of the unknown just as the little dark eyes of Ana Maria. It seemed I could see also in the future some slight wrinkles of worry. Or was it only the imagination of a young 23-year-old father, barely out of his own childhood?

Whatever the case, in some mysterious and unexplained way, for I had no words to express what I felt, I trusted in God and in the little girl with the small shiny eyes. I would also trust two other people whom, without my knowledge at that time, were waiting to come to us from the other side of life. There was a veil hiding important mysteries of life from me at that moment. God didn't think it was the proper time to reveal things which at that time I still did not have "eyes to see". My eyes were then only to look…

Neither God nor my children have ever let me down, my kids have taught me a lot since the moment they were born. I believe, however, that things could have been easier if I had a book like this to help me. The reader now has this book and can use it to know what is going on.

But, if this were the case, I would not have had the pleasure of writing it and would not be today so grateful to God for having allowed me to do so. And also to Ana Maria, Marta and Gilberto for having taught me so many of the things which were mentioned in the book. Without them, many of these things would have been unnoticed to the less attentive eyes of the hurried traveler.

Chapter 2.
THINGS WE MUST UNLEARN

Children don't come with manuals the way home appliances do. We learn how to use appliances by reading their instruction manuals that tell us everything we need to know about their use. Besides, children don't come with warranties that one can present to the manufacturer or seller, along with the purchase receipt in case they show some manufacturing defect and need to be exchanged.

There is a joke about a young father who had just taken his wife and baby son home from the hospital and a few hours later returned to complain that the baby was leaking.

Over time, people learn how to solve small problems that normally come up as well as big problems, if and when they come up. We count on the experience of our elders, normally one or both grandmothers, aunts, neighbors and especially doctors, to help us.

To make things easier I bought a book written by a famous pediatrician that I used in place of the manuals that come with home appliances and cars, hoping to fix or avoid the most common problems. In the book we are carefully taught how to take care of the new-born during its first days: how to bathe it, how to put it to sleep, how to dress and feed it, as well as how to understand certain typical signs that mark the different phases of its development: its first steps, teething, weight & growth progress, how to keep it clean and other information.

The purpose of these instructions is to help parents to bring up a healthy child so that the child may develop positive qualities such as intelligence, vitality and good manners. In other words, it aims at helping parents to raise children who will become persons useful to themselves and to the world where they are learning to live in.

Besides, the intention is to teach parents how to deal with the different situations children face at school, in life as a family, at work, with friends and in every different aspect of life.

All this is very important. Parents should offer their children, the elements that allow a child to live a decent, well-balanced, normal and happy life. This, however, is only part of the problem, because quite a few questions asked by fathers and mothers remain unanswered. There are books based on the knowledge of obstetricians, pediatricians, psychiatrists and psychologists but it is not common to find a book written with the experience of "spiritatrists"

We are told what to feed a child, how often it should take a bath, what kind of formula it should be fed. We learn whether the windows should be left open, if we should take it out in the sun or what we should give it in case it gets sick. There are different opinions on the subject but we can make our personal choices according to our needs and to those of the child. We end up giving it the food that most "agrees" with it, as the Americans would put it, the amount of rest and activity it requires, the clothes that fit the child best. But what could be said about the child itself, as a human being, as an individual? Why is the child temperamental or too quiet? What makes it calm or makes it nervous? Why does it like some people and dislike others? Why does it cry so much or not at all? Why does it take so long to talk or walk or to learn how to read? And later, why does our kid like math and not languages or the other way around? And above all, when you have two or more children, why are they so different despite being generated from the same set of genes and raised in the same home and in the same way?

After all who are our children? What do they mean to us and what do we mean to them, apart from the obvious parent/child relationship?

We still don't have clear and objective answers or, at least, ideas, to guide us in our daily struggles and joys. What we do have are preconceived and deeply-rooted ideas that have received the status of unquestionable truths that most of us accept without giving them much thought.

We could use this story as an example: Marquinhos has his mother's strong personality. Monica has her father's intelligence and her aunt's talent for art, or still her grandmother Adelaide's personality.

The first thing to "unlearn" about children is that they do not inherit personality traits such as intelligence, artistic inclinations, good or bad taste, charm, sweetness or aggressiveness. Each human being is unique in its psychological makeup, in its likes, its talents and personality. Only physical characteristics are genetically

CHAPTER 2.

transmitted such as: skin type, hair and eye color, body shape, predisposition to certain diseases etc. In all other aspects there is no genetic inheritance. Extremely bright parents can give birth to average children and not very gifted parents can have bright children. Calm parents can bear aggressive children and the other way around. Unstable parents may have excellent, well-balanced and sensible children. Anyone of us will be able to list at least five cases that prove what is being said here. That is why I am going to repeat that each child, each person is unique and although two or more people may share similar character traits, or even be very much alike, each person is totally unique, a true individual. Even identical twins, who share the same egg, display fundamental personality differences which make them totally unique.

It is important to stress that parents only produce the physical bodies of their children, not their spirits or souls. There is something else we must "unlearn" immediately so that we can open our minds to new ideas that are more intelligent, more rational and correct about some aspects of life: these spirits or souls that are entrusted to us, packed in the physical body we produced for them when they were conceived, are not brand-new beings, without a past or personal history. They existed somewhere before. They have their own personal stories and experiences, they are being reborn, not just being born.

It has been surprisingly difficult for people to accept this simple idea, amazing how they react strongly against it. Christ Himself said that John, the Baptist, was the reincarnation of the prophet Elias, although he was not recognized by his peers as such. In a different text Christ is surprised that Nicodemus, a respected member of the Sanhedrin ignored such an elementary truth that states that being reborn was important in order to achieve spiritual peace, which Jesus called Kingdom of God or Kingdom of Heaven.

This is therefore the pure, simple and unquestionable truth: our children, as well as ourselves, are human beings who have lived other lives. They bring a distant or not so distant baggage of experiences, mistakes, accomplishments and must follow a plan in the new life they are resuming. In the same way that we don't vanish into thin air when we die, we don't materialize out of nothing when we are reborn in a physical body. Everything continues; periods that follow others in cycles – here and beyond. So, write this down: we are all children created by God a long, long time ago and not new creatures created at the moment of conception or at the moment of birth to occupy a new physical body.

This idea is the main-stay of the architecture of life, the main concept that leads us to an understanding of its enigmas, its mysteries and its immortal beauty. It is, therefore, this idea, this concept, this truth that we chose as the foundation for this book, so that we can organize what we must know – within human limits – to understand life and also to help those around us understand it better. Everything, but really everything that goes against this truth, must be unlearned if we are truly to transform our lives into an intelligent evolutionary project that is the path towards spiritual perfection.

If your great-grandfather Joaquim was always critical and moody and he was reborn as your child you will probably have a slightly difficult and impatient child (unless he has changed during his experience outside the flesh). This happens in the same way that if an easygoing, peaceful person is reborn as your son or daughter you will have a serene, good-tempered and charming child from the moment it is born, although sometimes it will cry loudly if it's hungry, too hot, too cold or because its diapers need changing.

In what other way could it make you understand its needs? If it could talk it would ask you politely "Mummy, could you please change my diapers?" or "Aren't you forgetting my 10 o'clock bottle?"

Here's some advice to help you take care of your baby: it has got an adult intelligence and mature spirit trapped in small, immature physical body which does not allow it to express itself fully. This will come with time, you'll see, as the child grows up and becomes an adult. When it grows up it will be well to say that the child takes after its bad-tempered great-grandfather because, in fact, it can very well be the great-grandfather himself who was reborn. If the child is that distant bright relative who wrote books, or wrote music or if it is that great politician, then you will have the privilege and the responsibility of helping your child to express itself again as a human-being, probably in a different field of activity. In fact you will always have a great responsibility towards your children, whether they are girls or boys, smart or handicapped, easygoing or aggressive, healthy or sickly, calm or rebellious. For some reason, which you will one day understand, a child has been handed to you, or attracted or invited by you to come to this world. It will almost never be a total stranger, whose paths have never crossed yours in the past. Don't forget that you are a reborn spirit yourself.

Chapter 3.
HOW TO REORDER YOUR THOUGHTS

We have seen that the idea of rebirth will be used in this book as a way to reorder our thoughts on life. Now let us look into some of the things we have to unlearn to make space in our minds for what we have to relearn.

For example, we look at a little baby and immediately say: it looks like an angel, it's so innocent! It might even be a sweet and selfless angel, so wise and innocent in very rare occasions, a being that is very close to innocence, if we define innocence as the absence of malice, not the purity of one who has never made a mistake. Innocence cannot be used to define someone who has never made a mistake but one who has redeemed itself for the mistakes it has made, one who has overcome its bad tendencies and its difficulties and has reached the Kingdom of God, which is the construction of peace within ourselves.

A child is a spirit which has been entrusted to us for some time. It is seldom someone who is morally perfect and finished. Nor is it, with few exceptions, an evil demon. Angels and devils are opposites and they don't hang around with each other as some seem to think. A spirit who lives many wrongful lives and insists on making deliberate mistakes will fall so deeply into the bottom of the human scale that the process of reverting this situation will be very painful and long. The task of conquering peace is difficult although not impossible.

There are no such things as angels or devils, only creatures who have bettered themselves or who have gone astray, but have continued to be human beings. The souls or spirits summoned to give life to the physical bodies of our children are beings that are evolving, as we are ourselves, and to whom we are tied for this or that reason.

Sooner or later we all die, this is an undeniable truth. As we all know, the disposable physical body dies and is buried, cremated or whatever, while its spirit departs to the other side of life. After some time – a few years or sometimes centuries – when we return to earth to a new birth in another body, will we be angels of purity or evil demons only because we have come back in the flesh as a child? Not at all. We are what we have accumulated as baggage from past lives. Nevertheless, we are going to be limited by a physical body still in the process of development even after it leaves the mother's womb. The child will have to re-learn its new life under new circumstances and conditions. It will have to get used to the small body it has been given, learn the language of its new people and master manual skills such as drawing and writing as well as operating tools and using gadgets. It will have, thus, to adapt to the environment it has come to live in, as well as to the people sharing its new life: parents, siblings, relatives, neighbors, friends, etc, many of which may have been acquaintances from past lives. This process of re-learning is necessary because conscious memories of the past will begin to fade, as the spirit begins to awake in its new physical body. The consciousness of one side of life is normally turned on when that of the former side is turned off. It is like having two lights linked to only one switch, as one goes on, the other, automatically goes off. To remember past lives one has to be dreaming or unconscious. In those moments, consciousness is not present. It is necessary to be disconnected from one's physical body. In fact, it is not that our conscious mind is turned off on one side to be turned on in the other. What happens is that consciousness follows the spirit, which has the habit of partially and temporarily disconnecting itself from the physical body that is being used as shelter and as an instrument. This is one more piece of information we should bear in mind when dealing with a child during its learning years, or as Plato says its re-learning years for, according to the philosopher, to learn is to remember what we already knew in past lives.

Chapter 4.
RESPONSIBILITY

When it comes to responsibility, it is important to add that one should have a responsible attitude towards the child not only when it is born but from the moment it is conceived. Actually, both motherhood and fatherhood demand a minimum preparation that cannot be achieved in just a few months.

The decision of bearing a child which is able to shelter and serve a spirit is not one to be taken lightly. In fact, it happens to be a formal invitation to someone who already exists in a dimension beyond our usual senses. We need to welcome, raise and educate this child and give it a new opportunity for life. A baby should not be the result of a moment of carelessness. A man and a woman, usually young, when they get together, even if only once, should know a new life can result from that brief experience. Are there reasonable conditions to receive and care for this new person for the next twenty years? Above all: is this child welcome? Is there room for it in the hearts of those bringing it back to an earthly life?

There must be a minimum set of conditions for this child to come back, if not two outcomes are possible: the rejection of the child even before it is born in its mother's womb or, or its elimination by means of an abortion. The child will be considered an undesired "accident".

If it isn't wanted or if the parents feel they are not prepared to be parents because they lack the necessary psychological or financial means to do so then they should have thought of it *before* not after it is on the way.

It is very wrong to show hostility, negativity or rejection towards an unborn child. Whatever the circumstances are when a pregnancy begins there must be a strong reason for that spirit to inhabit the physical body inside the womb of its future mother. It is likely that it is someone previously linked to her or to its father or sometimes to both. The baby is a living thing that will surely play a very important role in its parents' lives. Conceiving a child may result from an irresponsible affair but the spirit that will come to live in this body isn't the result of chance – it is a pre-existing human being preparing itself to live again in the flesh. Do not send it back or hurt it with negative thoughts of lack of love. If people are able to make babies they should be able to have them. They should be mature enough to assume, even if alone, the consequences of their initial impulse.

We are going to repeat here – and we shall do it to exhaustion - a child is a human being, with rights, obligations, responsibilities and plans, such as you, me and everyone else. Do not think of it as a mere fetus, a "thing". On the contrary, it is a person, the same way you are.

Very seldom will it be possible to find out, with enough precision, who that person is and how were you linked in the past. It can be a good friend from the past, coming to profess its love for you. It might be coming to help you in the difficult task of life, to keep you company when old age comes about, or even to help you financially.

It is also true that it can be a former enemy that is angry or upset at what you did to him or her in another life. But it is coming to attempt reconciliation so that you can forgive each other and from then on continue as friends, or at least peacefully, no longer as enemies.

Whatever the situation, it is not a coincidence that that spirit approaches you looking for an opportunity to live a new life. In one way or the other, it is up to the parents to take full responsibility for what they caused in a conscious or inconsequent way, the conception of a new being.

I have many stories regarding this subject but, for the sake of brevity, I have chosen a few to illustrate my point. These stories are all authentic, there is not a word of fiction here.

Case A – The newly-married daughter of a friend of mine was having pregnancy problems. Although she badly wanted a child her pregnancies always ended up in miscarriage. It seemed the spirit or spirits to be incarnated in her future baby was feeling insecure or afraid. As a result of my work with a group of mediums, I found out a little about that family's past lives. In the 16th century Europe, my friend, the father of the expecting mother, had a pretty important political status. For unknown reasons an acquaintance had trusted him with the task of raising and educating his daughter. It isn't clear why but the task he was given was not performed successfully which

CHAPTER 4.

made the girl's father very unhappy. When all these people died the situation was seemingly solved from the carnal point of view. That, however, isn't the way things work out beyond our five insufficient senses.

After a long time, centuries in this case, the girl who was raised by the eminent European politician was reborn as his own daughter and they all live in present day Brazil. It is possible that since he did not perform his duties as promised nearly four centuries before, he had now decided to be a father. But this time, it was the former father's turn to be reborn as the son of his former daughter and consequently as a grandson of the man who had broken his trust. Are you following the plot?

This was the scheme conceived to solve the conflict among these people, which seemed without solution. The problem is that the former father, who had trusted his daughter to his present grandfather to be, was still so hurt that he now was in doubt whether to accept him as his grandfather. Wouldn´t he make him suffer again?

Meanwhile my friend's daughter was again pregnant and was in risk of losing the baby. As I indirectly knew the reasons for these problems, I sent a subtle message to my friend who perfectly understood it. In this message I told him that the spirit to be incarnated in his future grandson was afraid to do so because of the problems he had had with him in a past life. I told him to mentally talk to the spirit reassuring it that all past problems had been settled and that it would be welcome with joy and love. "Tell him to have faith and to come in peace." From then on everything seemed to work out well. A strong and healthy boy was born and the grandfather says they get along very well.

Case B: This case was described in a book written by my very dear friend dr. Jorge Andréa dos Santos, a renowned physician, writer, lecturer and researcher. It is the true story of a middle-aged couple who had decided they had already brought enough children into this world and therefore wanted to cancel all new "invitations" for future incarnations. The next step was to have the woman's tubes tied although she still had many fertile years ahead of her.

What happened is that on the day of the surgery, one of the surgeons was unable to attend and the lady´s husband, a surgeon himself, was asked to fill in for him in the operating room. He therefore witnessed all of the surgical procedures and saw the fallopian tubes being cut and tied. Pregnancy would be impossible after such a radical procedure. But was it really impossible? No one knows what happened, but the fact is that the lady became pregnant again. It seems that "someone" performed an efficient "invisible" surgery to restore her tubes, making them functional again, so that one more spirit could return to flesh.

Jorge Andréa, a witness in this case, knows who this child was in his previous life.

He had long conversations with it, while the child was "only" a spirit on the other side of life.

In fact many of these understandings and "negotiations" occur on invisible levels between future parents and future children. In these negotiations previous relationships can continue in future lives. If everything goes well and all the parties act wisely, as my own mother used to teach us, the future will be better. But if the conditions for the relationship are rejected or aggravated, then much pain and maladjustment is to be expected.

Case A is not a typical example of rejection on the part of a father or a mother or much less of a grandfather. It was the spirit about to return to the flesh that was afraid of facing difficulties it imagined could come about in its future life. In Case B, narrated by Jorge Andréa – the opposite happens - it was not rejection since the spirit was received with love, and is being treated with much affection and respect due to the exceptional conditions under which it was born. It was only an example of the unexpected, the means used by invisible forces when they deem it is necessary. It can be said that there was interference in the couple's free will, as they had apparently decided not to have more children. But who can say they did not unconsciously agree to make an exception?

In Dr. Helen Wambach's book, "Life before Life", we can find many examples of reborn spirits that felt truly rejected. It is important to mention that this famous American psychologist used to submit her patients to memory regression sessions and was able to take them back to pre-natal stages, where she collected very interesting statements, as we will later see in this book. (She died in 1985).

"...I knew for sure" (says one person), "that my mother didn't want me, and I was surprised and disappointed."

CHAPTER 4.

"...I know my mother was ashamed of me because I was an ugly baby."

"...I knew my mother didn't really want me because of the heavy burden I would place on her. In fact, I was only able to realize how unfortunate my birth was after this memory regression procedure."

"...I feared the future ahead of me. I felt that the doctors taking care of my mother were cold and detached. They weren't sympathetic towards my mother´s pains and fears. I can remember how I suffered in this cold environment."

These are some dramatic examples of how babies are people like us, since the first instant of life. After all, it is not the first moment but only a moment in the continuity of life. Life is not a still pond but a constant flow of a river.

We mentioned two possible outcomes of unwanted pregnancies. Rejection has serious consequences as we have seen. The other act is not only disastrous but also a crime: it is called abortion.

We shall deal with it in the next chapter.

Chapter 5.
A FLASK OF POISON

If one replaces the label from a poison bottle for another label saying *drinking water*, it will still be poison, still be a lethal substance. Therefore let's avoid euphemisms and misleading words that attempt to hide the ugly and concrete truth: abortion is premeditated murder. It will never be ignored by the divine laws that rule the universe. Nevertheless we should never forget that these same laws provide the necessary means to correct our mistakes.

The body of a fetus, even when it is just a cluster of cells, holds an adult and conscious spirit, carrying many past experiences from former earthly lives. If one interferes with the formation process of that little body, the spirit destined to inhabit it, even though not yet totally linked to the fetus, will feel the brutal impact of violence and rejection, both physically and emotionally speaking. This would be like slamming the door on a dear one's face, a friend who has come to ask you for help on a cold stormy night, looking for shelter, food and love; things you actually owe this person.

An abortion will usually lead to a series of tragic events for the mother or the parents who rejected the spirit that was about to be reborn and for the spirit itself. The spirit will suffer the most specially if it still remains in a state of emotional or mental unbalance.

If the spirit is calm, well balanced and affectionate, the consequences might be minimized, although never ignored by the divine laws. If, on the other hand, the spirit is bitter and prone to violence and, as it occurs with frequency, the faulty parents owe the spirit some sort of reparation, usually a process of conflict, persecution, revenge and awakening of old resentments takes place, coming back with renewed intensity

Situations such as these can last for centuries, until the people involved finally realize the significance of brotherly love. The only way out of the conflicts caused by an abortion is love, understanding and acceptance. Problems that could have been solved, not easily but

CHAPTER 5.

with a good chance of success, may continue, become worse or more serious than ever.

An abortion is a serious mistake. The person who undergoes the procedure, or her male partner with his direct or indirect influence, or the professionals that perform it, are all involved in practicing a crime against a person who can't defend itself or escape and are guilty of shamefully destroying a human life. That spirit remains alive as spirits are immortal. What happens is that the spirit has been denied the chance of returning to life on earth and of carrying out its mission here.

I have heard many dramatic stories concerning abortions. After many years of dealing and working with spirits in long relationships I have learned of amazing tragedies connected to abortions.

I have mentioned that an abortion is a bad decision and stated that there is an inevitable involvement with unpredictable consequences, in any abortive procedure. It is a fact that human laws admit and even promote abortions, but that does not mean that they are not crimes against the laws of nature and even more seriously against the laws of God. Those involved in an abortion are required to fix their mistakes so that cosmic harmony may be achieved.

People that get or perform abortions seem totally unaware and uninterested in the consequences of their acts and decisions. This is due to the fact that they ignore the depth and consequences of their acts or maybe that they insist on practicing such a crime even when they are aware of such consequences as the laws of men only punishes it if it is performed by unauthorized professionals. It is even said that the law became more "evolved" as it started accepting, or even stimulating what was formerly condemned: abortions without a justified reason may be performed by recognized medical professionals.

Non-religious or materialistic people don't have any regrets about ending a life that is just rehearsing its first steps in the carnal world. To such people a fetus is just a cluster of disposable cells as it is unable to think intelligently or to feel. In other words it is not a human being such as they know it. In addition, there are many who really do not believe in such things as the soul, the spirit, the afterlife and reincarnation and therefore are not concerned about the consequences of an abortion. To these people the death of a fetus or that of an adult is an inevitable accident that forever interrupts life.

The person just falls into a nonexistent darkness.

But the truth is quite different. For every rejected or aborted fetus there is a corresponding conscious, living, immortal spirit. Many times the little body, weighing no more than a few hundred grams, is soon forgotten after it is removed from its mother's womb, but the spirit who was intended for that body continues living consciously in some unknown dimension. It will be there waiting for those who have denied it the sacred opportunity of life, if not with an aggressive attitude, at least with a puzzled accusatory look or a dramatic silence of censorship or grief.

It is common for these spirits to start persecuting and tormenting the murderers of their would-be bodies even while these continue in their earthly existences to perform new abortions and therefore commit the same crimes against new spirits or against the same spirit which was again trying to be reborn.

This is one of the basic mistakes of those who perform abortions: to believe that once the fetus is removed they will be free from the problems caused by it.

But as I have previously mentioned, I have heard dramatic statements coming from spirits involved in such tragic mistakes. As we are short of space, we will choose an excerpt from an article published in the "Folha Espírita" (The Spiritual Journal), a publication from São Paulo where the readers can find the complete version.

The spirit who came to tell us the case was that of a woman. In a previous existence she had continuously had abortions every time she got pregnant. Because of her professional activities she felt that babies were just heavy loads that she needed to get rid of as soon as possible. How could she care for them? That would be a permanent sacrifice; day in day out, making her tired, old, spoiling her hands and specially her body which was her best asset. No way! It seemed to her that it was easier to get rid of the babies as soon as she got pregnant or as happened later, soon after they were born.

They were a total of eight. When she returned to the spiritual world, the day of her death, she met all of them. They were waiting for her and confronted her with unexpected hostility as they were extremely upset about her criminal acts which had interrupted their chances of a new life.

CHAPTER 5.

For a long time she was a victim of their hatred and aggressiveness for as Christ said, the man who practices a sin, is, in fact, a slave to that sin. One cannot leave until the last cent has been paid. This debt is the same as any debt in an earthly existence but in the spiritual plane even if one is willing to pay one will still have to go to jail. The debt will be paid with hard work, tears and difficulties so that one day the spirit will be able to smile after it has regained the trust of those it has sinned against.

To make a long story short the young woman was treated in the spiritual world, where she came to understand the extent of her mistakes. She accepted (did she have another way out?) the conditions which were *granted* to her as nothing is forced, unless in extreme cases. The conditions were the following: she would reincarnate as the eldest daughter of a poor family in Argentina. Her father would be a hopeless alcoholic (she herself was the one who had led him to this in a previous existence). Her mother would have to give birth to all of the eight spirits she had denied the chance to be reborn, and they would be her siblings. Her mother would then die, leaving her with the task of raising and supporting her eight siblings with the product of her sweat and hard work as well as caring for her drunken father, a former lover in a past life whom she had also rejected.

She would be attractive and healthy but her situation would keep her from getting married although she would be tempted to do so by more than one suitor. If she did she would affect all of the initial arrangement. Her task was to bring up the children she had previously rejected.

Such a task would have been easier in her previous incarnation when she had been better off financially. Now it would have to be done truly at the cost of blood, sweat and tears because her present siblings, with one exception, saw her as the mother who had murdered them in her previous life and not as the caring sister who was capable of any sacrifice in her struggle to make all of them survive honestly.

To carry out this very difficult redeeming task she counted on two helpers: her mother, a long time spiritual partner (who had been her mother in a previous life) and who had volunteered to give birth to the children she had rejected in her previous incarnation, and her eldest brother, who despite having been rejected too, bore no grudges against her as he was a well-adjusted and evolved spirit.

When this whole scheme had been explained to her she asked: - "Why can't I get married like everyone else and give birth to these children with the help of a husband, instead of raising them as troublesome siblings who are so vengeful and hostile?"

The answer was that this would not be possible firstly because it was her duty to raise these children with the means provided by her own hard work, not with the means provided by a husband. Secondly, the spirits of the children she had rejected were still so angry and offended that they could never survive in her womb. In the presence of such rejection between mother and babies, miscarriages are bound to happen and this would frustrate the reconciliation plans.

The woman in this case was faced with an unsolvable problem. She could refuse this plan, as she could exercise her free will, but this would only postpone matters and things would become increasingly harder. How long could she postpone this situation? Could it be a century, four hundred years or a thousand years? Besides, when would it be possible to reunite the characters of this tragic story and lead them towards making amends?

There was no other acceptable or easier solution. The woman took a deep breath and accepted her ordeal. Before her were images of a future that already existed but had yet to be lived. She could see it and feel it in her hands that rough and exhaustive work would make coarse, in her beautiful body that would be deformed by hard work, in her frustrations, anxieties and abdications, in her disgust for a life in which she would be a prisoner, tied down by the weight of so many responsibilities and aggravated by the hatred and ungratefulness of her hostile siblings who were always demanding more than she could give them. She would, in the future, suffer the agony and loneliness of living among so many people who hated her. And it would be up to her to transform all these negative feelings into love, understanding and forgiveness.

This is a dear friend's story. She cried with me a tear of regret and smiled with hope. We parted as father and daughter for this was her wish. She wished she could, if not be reborn as my daughter at least find me here where I would be able to help her to cope with her difficulties. She has great trust in me and in my spiritual companions. I would open my heart to her because her story really touched me, but she had a plan to fulfill and I could see a wonderful ray of hope in her future.

CHAPTER 5.

If the reader has a moment, please say a prayer for her to help her in her struggle.

***

I must add that this story was written and published at the request of that woman's spirit hoping that other women could take into account the tragedies that can result from an abortion.

I do, however, reinforce my words by saying that the divine laws are always ready to grant us the opportunity to redeem ourselves because they are educational and not punitive, but indeed, very strict.

Chapter 6.
TODAY OR MANY HALLEYS FROM NOW?

The reader who is not familiar with certain concepts that are exposed here such as spirit, soul, rebirth, immortality and so on, may very well think that what I am doing is propaganda of my ideas, leaving the task of explaining the great mysteries of human life such as giving birth, raising and educating a child in second place." This is not but spiritist preaching", you may be thinking

Let us clarify this point before going on.

In fact, I am a spiritist, but that is not why I am writing these things. I am doing so because I believe truth is exactly so, and it wouldn't be honest to believe something and write another. I am also a father and my children have their mother and they are beginning to have their own children: my grandchildren. I know how important these things are and that they should not, under any circumstances, be the object of uneducated speculation, petty lies or half-truths. The truth of the matter is that your children, as well as my own, are real people, spirits that have existed before and that will continue to exist after we die and they themselves die. I even understand that you may not be ready to agree with me on this point. It doesn't matter. This won't be the end of our friendship. Neither will we lose respect for each other because of this. This wouldn't help us anyway. If it were all a lie, I would have nothing to gain by it. But if it's true, as it is, it won't make a difference if you believe in it or not, accept it or not, or agree or disagree, one day truth will come out and, as our Paul said, truth is as pacient as charity.

It's true that for more than a century spiritists have been the only ones to talk about things such as reincarnation, for example. But this is not a new idea and it was not invented by Mr.Allan Kardec. I can assure you that Prof.Rivail (his real name) took some time to accept this idea that seemed very strange to him at first. But, as I have said before, when something is really true it will be recognized as such in the end. As Professor Rivail was an educated and intelligent man, it was easier and faster for him to accept the truth than it would have been for a less prepared person. Truth is always an intelligent thing and the longer we take to acknowledge it, the longer we will wander through the paths of life. It may take years or centuries but one day we will end up seeing the light and then, looking back, we may very well say: "My God, so much time has been wasted!"

And we will stop and realize that it will be better to start working immediately since that task that could already have been concluded many, many moons ago... Or maybe many Halleys ago, once each four Halleys sum up nearly 300 years or, more precisely, every 304 years...

My suggestion to the reader: you have every right to reject all of my ideas, to close this book or even to get rid of it, but, if you do, remember the day you made this decision as you will, sometime in the future, regret it. Somewhere in an unforeseen intersection of time and space this decision will be remembered and it won't be a happy moment as you will be very angry at yourself. And there is one more thing: if you really decide to throw this book out, do it in such a way as to allow someone else to find it as it might find its way into the hands of someone who is more prepared to accept the truth than you were.

To sum it up, it doesn't matter whether it is a spiritist idea or not but whether it is the truth or a lie. I, among others, say that it is true.

Nowadays it is not only spiritists who believe these truths and this is exactly where I wanted to get.

Let us leave spiritist literature aside for a moment and focus on Dr. Helen Wambach's book which I have briefly mentioned before.

But firstly let me say that Helen Wambach is an American psychologist with a PhD, whom, through the use of past life regression therapy, was able to gather the most important records of scientific data on past lives to date.

Memory regressions are performed with the patient who is under a hypnotic or magnetic trance and is then led back in time in search of past memories. The patient will start with recent memories and then go back to his youth, childhood, life in his mother's womb, his life as a spirit and finally to previous lives or incarnations in this great world of God.

The reader may find more information in the book I wrote "Memory and Time", where this theme is covered in depth. It will allow for a greater understanding of this subject which is too long to be disclosed here.

The technique employed by Dr. Wambach involves "reducing the electrical potential of a patient's brainwaves to five cycles per second." According to her, although the patient is not fully aware of what it is all about his "internal mind" is. I would say that it is the spirit who knows but this is not very important right now.

After the patient has reached the desired point in the therapy she begins her elaborate technique of collecting data.

It is about her book "Life before life" that we are going to talk in the following chapters, since as we have agreed, you the reader, and I the author, to give priority to data not from spiritist literature but coming exclusively from scientific books.

Chapter 7.
BEING BORN IS THE PROBLEM, NOT DYING

The excellent survey done by Dr. Wambach was based on the following questions that were asked to the hypnotized patients when they reached the period immediately before their birth:

1) Being born, was it your own decision?

2) Did anyone help you decide? If so, what was your relationship with that person?

3) What is your expectation about living your next existence?

4) Was there any reason for you to have decided to live in the second half of the twentieth century?

5) Was it you who chose your sex? If so, what led you to decide to be born a man or a woman?

6) What is your main purpose in this life?

7) In case you had already met your mother in a previous life, what kind of relationship did you have with her?

8) What about your father? Had you two met before? If so, what kind of relationship did you have with him?

9) Concentrate on the fetus. Do you feel inside it or outside it? Do you feel like you are going in and out? When does your conscience become part of the fetus?

10) Are you aware of the attitudes and feelings your mother had for you just before you were born?

11) How did you feel as you came out of your mother's body?

One can easily notice that Dr. Wambach is not just imagining, or addressing a thing, an abstraction or a hypothesis. She is interviewing a normal, intelligent, conscious and responsible person who is capable of observing, concluding and expressing ideas correctly, in the way normal adults can. She is not talking to a newborn baby with no previous memories, who is unable to have any type of relationship with its mother, father or any other person.

It is a human being who is able to answer whether it was its own choice to live another incarnated life or whether it was led (or even forced) to that decision. It can remember the people with whom it discussed and programmed its life and helped it to elaborate its objectives, its needs and projects for the new life. The spirit that is going to be born is someone who seriously considered the responsibilities of a new existence; someone who decided to be born at a certain time, not before or after that time; someone who decided what sex it would have as a result of a conscious choice. It is someone who had usually known its parents from previous lives, and who had family ties with them, or been friends or even had quarrels which have to be settled. It is a spirit who is aware of being linked to a fetus, i.e. to a physical body in formation.

Moreover, these spirits somehow know, in a still inexplicable way, what feelings their future mothers, fathers, and other people had for them.

Finally it is able to observe the process in its totality, to analyze it clearly and to conclude, in an organized way, what its opinion of the whole process is.

I believe we should spend more time on this scientific data, as it is too important to be considered in just two or three quick sentences. The information resulting from this research is extremely important to us all and that is why I intend to return to it later in this book. But, before that, it seems appropriate to examine some statistical data collected by the very brilliant Dr. Helen Wambach.

Ninety percent of the patients who were submitted to regression therapy brought back surprises to themselves and to Dr. Wambach. One of these is that dying is good but being born isn't very interesting. "The two deaths I experienced, in the two lives I remembered this evening, were very pleasant," writes a patient. "Being born was hard."

Who would ever have thought?

Another unexpected piece of information collected by Dr. Wambach: none of her 750 patients, at that point in her research, felt that "their true inner self was male or female." This will lead to the proof mentioned in my book Spirituality and Human Problems that libido is a form of energy, and that gender results from a polarization of this energy.

Another surprising finding is that the consciousness in every human being does not come from the fetus. It is not an integral part of it, but is just in it. "The spirits exist and are completely conscious independently of the fetus". In fact, the fetal body is restrictive and binding and many would prefer "the freedom of *existing without* a body." In other words, it would have been better not being born at all.

The newborn baby "feels secluded, confined and lonely as compared to how it felt while in the intermediary state between one life and the other."

Let's return to the statistical data:

1) 81 % of the patients declared that the decision to be reborn was their own. 19% said they did not remember or had had no opinion regarding this matter.

2) Of the total surveyed, 68% informed they were uptight or unwilling to accept the perspective of a new life. Only 26% considered the possibility with fair optimism, and these did not seek a life of pleasures, but a life that would allow them to evolve spiritually.

3) 90% of the patients in the survey stated that their deaths were pleasant experiences, whereas their births caused them suffering and apprehension.

4) Concerning the goals and plans for the lives ahead of them, the researcher did not detect any projects aimed at developing talents and gifts, but a general "priority of learning to deal with people in a better way and to love without being demanding or possessive." In this group, 28% were aware of having brought a "message" to mankind, stressing the importance of solidarity with one's fellow men and "the development of a superior conscience", that is, the firm belief that we are all mainly spiritual beings. Dr.Wambach's patients were "practically unanimous in rejecting any intentions of getting richer or gaining more status."

5) 87% of the subjects, a very high average, informed they had known their parents, lovers and friends from one or other previous lives. The researcher did not find any clues suggesting the Freudian theories of the so-called Oedipus and Electra complexes, by which it is expected that sons are attracted sexually to their mothers and girls to their fathers. (This subject can be found in my book "Memory and Time"). Previous relationship may have been very, very diversified.

As we can conclude from all of the above, being reborn is still, for most people, a hard experience, more a duty than a pleasure. On the other hand, dying is a process that frees a person from the prison of the flesh.

But the most essential and dramatic finding in this scientific research, is that each child is an adult spiritual being who is experienced, conscious and has much knowledge. The spirit is the author of a deliberate life project involving goals, objectives and proposals that are clearly conceived and planned in advance. A child is, therefore, a pre-existent survivor, just as spiritists have been teaching for over a century and as Christ Himself taught two thousand years ago.

I think, however, that we still have important aspects to learn from the excellent work performed by Dr. Helen Wambach in her careful scientific research.

Is the reader still with me? Shall we go on? Or did you decide to throw away this book, and I didn´t notice when you got off the train? If you did, never mind. But I'm sorry to tell you that you will have to stand there, waiting for another train to come and it can take much longer than you think. But, it is obvious, that it's up to you and you have every right to exercise your free will.

Chapter 8.
WHAT ARE WE BORN FOR?

As it is impossible to comment all of Dr. Wambach's book because it would involve writing a whole new book I decided to choose and summarize two or three points that are part of it and seem especially important to support our own work. The time chosen, for instance. Why had all these people chosen to be reborn in the second half of the twentieth century?

There can be a wide variety of answers to this question, but one can say that this time was chosen because great expectations for spiritual growth were in store. Man is beginning to understand himself, his immortality and his capability of reaching perfection. Among all subjects surveyed 51% stated that they were born during this period "because of its great potential for human spiritual growth". Some said that many highly developed spirits are being reborn now, and "we are all approaching world peace, and a general understanding of mankind as one." Or that "many great souls are coming together" for the creation of a "Golden Age" in which "monumental changes are beginning to occur, and will continue to take shape."

In fact, most subjects were optimistic about world affairs, even though there was still a small, inexpressive percentage of 4 out of 100 that were pessimistic about the period they had chosen to be born in.

Many, however, had decided to come because of their connections to other people who were living at that time or who were supposed to be born at the same time. Among other reasons were the search for understanding, the settlement of former grudges, or the intention of dedicating oneself to someone or to mankind. A woman declared she was sure of having been born to "give birth to a political leader."

Many women declared they had chosen to be born in this period in history because many social changes were in store for them, not only as far as more freedom for women but mainly a considerable upgrade in their *status*.

As for the choice of gender, there were many reasons worthy of consideration.

> I chose to be a woman (said one girl) because women are more affectionate, expressive and self-connected. I feel *my feminine side* is better suited to show these feelings (my italics).

Another man gave the following reason for his choice:

> Well, I really didn't choose my sex, but I was glad to find out that this time I would be a man. I was a woman in most of my lives, and this was the cause of great suffering for me.

As for the objectives and reasons for a new life, the unquestionable main tone is the chance to learn, or better, to relearn brotherly love. It is amazing that, among so many different people, so different from each other there is such a coincidence of thoughts.

> When you asked what the purpose of my life is I realized that it is to improve my relationship with people I hurt in past lives and to whom I owe reparations. I am now sure that my purpose is to help my alcoholic husband to whom I was very cruel in a previous life.

Or ...my task was to make amends with all the people I have hurt in past lives.

Here are Dr.Wambach's comments on these statements:

> (...) 18% of my patients said they had come to life on Earth to learn to spread love. Their motivation was not to be with specific people, but *to learn to love.* (my italics)

Someone said: "I must stop being so possessive."

There were people saying they came "to rid themselves of materialism and to stop being negative towards life", as well as "to combine male and female emotional traits" and to develop the control over love, character strength and such emotional traits. Imagine if one of these people that were born under the pressure of disconnected impulses exactly to learn how to control tumultuous passions, meets a bad advisor who stimulates them to assume their latent homosexuality, for example.

According to Dr.Wambach's research, there are different opinions regarding the exact moment the spirit joins the fetus. Some say it happens at the moment of conception, but others only felt this connection after being born and even with certain freedom to move out of the body. Dr.Wambach's research shows that 89% of the 750 subjects who underwent the survey up to the time the book was published in March, 1979 said that they only felt the true body/spirit connection after they had been in their mother's womb for 6 months.

I have no reason to doubt these results but I believe that there might be a difference between what the person *remembers* and what actually *happened*. The general rule is that in the first few weeks in the pregnancy a fetus has been appointed a spirit who is being prepared to be born again.

Dr. Jorge Andréa believes that the spirit may even be present and influence the choice of the specific sperm which will trigger the fertilization process and the resulting pregnancy. It is clear, however, that in order for this to happen the spirit must be evolved and wise as there are situations which are decided based on emergencies that don't allow spirits to participate at all in such decisions. Nevertheless, it is obvious that the spirit's participation is very important especially when it comes to this connection with the fetus as it is the perispirit that brings the karmic structures that will decide how this new physical body will be, affecting the purely genetic mechanisms.

Those who have committed suicides in former lives have talked about this process and their bodies have physical signs of damage in the place the suicide was attempted. If a person shot their ears, hearts, lungs or stomach there will be a mark showing where the damage was done because it was done to their spiritual mold. If they drowned or choked or poisoned themselves there will be physical signs on their bodies showing this.

Likewise, the Divine Laws that rule everything with wisdom will provide human beings who don't need to perform reparations with a body which will enable them to fulfill their mission here on Earth. They will receive a good physical brain, skillful hands or the health that will assure them the years of life they will need to perform such chores.

It is clear that there must be a relationship between this and the parents' genetic makeup. This shows us how complex and delicate the operations that take place backstage of something apparently so simple and automatic as the conception of a child are. Yes, because, in fact, the mechanism of fecundation itself requires no special competence or knowledge from the parents, many of whom do not have the faintest idea of the unconceivable complexity behind the laws and processes regarding this perfect event. The mechanism starts working as soon as the "negotiations" begin to happen in the world invisible to our eyes. Such negotiations involve enabling a spiritual group to be born at the same time while following an organized schedule, with well-defined relationships and specific tasks. Nothing is left to chance or improvisation, although there is flexibility in terms of certain choices. What makes this matter complicated is the fact that many who arrive here fail to do the share of the work assigned to them and this brings lots of confusion and further suffering.

These previous settlements and plannings are of an impressive realism. Dr. Wambach, mentioned the story of a spirit who was about to be born whom, having noticed that his mother to be was considering to get rid of him by performing an abortion, had a serious talk with her on a spiritual level and managed to dissuade her from performing her wrongful act.

Another person told Dr.Wambach an interesting story I would like to share with you as it contains important lessons.

Chapter 9.
REFLEXIONS ON ADOPTION

In order to understand certain aspects of her personality, a woman who had gone back twice to the time before she was born, through the process of regression, said the following:

"When I was still a spirit, between my former incarnation and the one for which I was preparing myself, I decided I would be born to a certain couple, as they had the best genetic properties that would allow me to have the physical and mental skills I desired. But I also knew that there was another couple that was in a better position to provide me with the education I wanted. Therefore, the plan was to be born to a couple and to be adopted by another. The plan also involved being born a boy, although this did not happen due to my impatience"

(Lesson 1: Impatience and outrage impulses, even when rare or apparently without consequences generally result in unforeseen and possibly complicated results.)

From the woman's account it is possible to tell that the couple that had been chosen to be her genetic parents was programmed to have two children, first a girl, and eighteen months later a boy. The second body was the one chosen by Dr. Wambach's patient.

But, in a gesture of impatience, she decided to take the first body, and ended up being born a girl and not a boy as she had wanted. And it was only during the regression she undertook that she finally understood why she felt so uncomfortable in a female body.

(Lesson 2: Sex changes can cause problems, some of them quite serious.)

***

Before we go on, I think it is necessary to clarify some points. (This observation was first made in the fourth edition of this book.)

As a consequence of having been written in a summarized and imprecise form the statement made in parenthesis as "Lesson 2" brought about doubts and protests from some readers concerned with the purity of the doctrine who imagined that I had admitted the possibility of an unborn spirit being able to change the sex of an unborn fetus, in that particular case from male to female. I have to admit that the way in which it was written might have given rise to this interpretation, but it is not what really happened. After carefully reading this chapter one will be able to note that this is a mistaken conclusion because the spirit's objective for reincarnation was precisely to be born in a male body. Even if she could, and if it were possible to change the fetus' sex, she wouldn't do it, because her intention was to be born a man.

I didn't mean to state that a change of sex is possible after a fetus has decided its sexual preference, but to call attention to the fact that some behavioral disturbances may occur when this change takes place from one incarnation to the other. In other words: after many lives as a male, a spirit may, although not necessarily, have some difficulty to adapt to life as a woman, and may even be tempted to become a homosexual. There are some brief but specific references about this subject in chapter 8 above (What are we born for?). The very girl who went through such experience, mentions the uneasiness she felt in the body of a woman when she would have preferred to have been reborn as a man.

If the reader is interested in more information on the subject please refer to the section called "A dualistic point view on sexuality problems", that I wrote for the book "Spiritism and Human Problems", pages 163 - 183 written by my late dear friend Deolindo Amorim.

***

After clarifying this point, let's go back to our story.

This change in plans had caused another unforeseen change: the foster parents had been "prepared" to receive a boy, not a girl. The young woman could not remember everything precisely, but she declared (truly, I believe) that "probably things had to be worked out" for *her* to be adopted and not her younger brother, whose body she had formerly chosen to be hers. This explanation seems to be correct, as it explains why the adopting parents who had been prepared to receive a boy, ended up adopting a girl, in spite of both children having been given up for adoption. (Lesson 3: an intense exchange of ideas, proposals and agreements occurs in the invisible world, although we are rarely aware of it.)

CHAPTER 9.

And this raises a problem which I had chosen to talk about later in this book but which fits into this part of the story.

Should people adopt?

This is a much more complicated matter than it seems to be at first glance. It is impossible to answer yes or no as it isn't a black and white question. As in many other areas in life the best answer isn't just a yes or a no.

The first aspect that should be considered is that of karma. I hope it is by now understood that spirits are reborn with well-established and detailed life plans, and that they are programmed to reach specific goals, especially those related to learning or relearning about the aspects of love, as we have seen before.

We are aware that the laws of God are at the same time strict and flexible and their purpose is *educational* not *punitive*. And, we know that the Divine Laws only impose bearable punishments that one can endure. If we take wealth for granted, for instance, we will surely live one or more lives having financial problems or being poor. If we use physical beauty as a weapon to get what we want, we can count on ugliness in future lives. If we take our health for granted there will be surely health problems in future existences. If we disdain true love, we will undoubtedly be abandoned, lonely and will not find love in a next existence (or even in more than one existence). The learning experience comes through the exchange of signs in the same measure, extension and content of the mistake that was made. No more no less, because when we make a mistake, we produce a "mold" that will be used in the reparation mechanisms. And that is why the word *karma* means action and reaction and, because of that, some authors call it the Law of Cause and Effect. These are different ways of explaining the same basic concept which is that you are responsible for everything you do wrong and have all your good deeds in your favor, no matter how insignificant they may be. Every point counts, one way or the other, negative or positive. The result of this balance is the measure of our inner peace or our emotional disturbances that still remain in us, awaiting for a solution.

It so happens that a spirit born under unfavorable conditions will certainly have a still unsolved situation to deal with as the law never imposes useless sacrifices on an innocent person. However, in spite of its fantastic complexity, the law is logical and paradoxically simple as to its results. As we have recently mentioned, it is not totally inflexible. The law does not get in the way of charity, much to the contrary, it always allows room for the exercise of the major virtue of love towards our neighbors at all times. This means we should not be indifferent in situations of pain and suffering just because we assume the persons involved made serious mistakes in the past and therefore deserve their present suffering. We should never refuse help to somebody who suffers, under the false idea that to learn that person has to suffer anyway. Anyone of us in a similar unfortunate situation would welcome gestures of solidarity, love and help in order to overcome suffering, even if we deserve this situation. Peter, the apostle said that "love covereth a multitude of sins".

Many times gestures of fraternal love and understanding will awaken in a suffering soul the strength to accept its difficult destiny without any resentment or revolt making it understand that the vast territories of happiness and peace lay not too far ahead. They lay *immediately past* the narrow path of thorns which is overcome through purifying pains.

But, returning to the subject at hand, what about adoption?

I have said before that there are no definitive, self-excluding, black or white type answers. The best rule in such cases is to follow one's intuition, seeking the answer in prayer or meditation and hearing the inner voice within oneself.

In my opinion (attention: my *personal opinion*, not a general rule), adoptions are the human solutions to dealing with newborns who have been abandoned by their mothers or children left to orphanages. As to children who belong to families afflicted by poverty and other difficulties, it is my opinion that they should be assisted, helped, supervised, oriented, but kept exactly where they are. Moving a child from an environment of poverty and simplicity to a rich and sophisticated one will bring about serious and unforeseen risks and inconveniences.

I think I should explain this point of view which is, I repeat, *my personal* opinion.

I did not have a firm opinion on this matter, until some time ago, when a spirit told our group that after one or two existences as someone who had it all, - beauty, fortune, social status, power- she had to live in extreme poverty, because when she had it all, she had used her gifts to make mistakes, to oppress others, to impose her will

CHAPTER 9.

on others, causing many people to suffer as a result.

Well, as she was born in a poor environment she was programmed to lead a difficult but honest life which would give her the chance to expiate her sins. But, as she was a very pretty little girl, someone took her away from that environment, and raised her once again in a life of wealth and luxury, where she was confronted again with her old spiritual "molds". She again made the same mistakes of her former incarnations. When she finally returned to spiritual life, her debts had been increased and aggravated, instead of being diminished or even abolished if she had led a poor life in her last incarnation.

While living, everything seemed fine. She was the poor girl that had ascended socially, and started a life as a great lady, using her beauty and supposed refinement and good manners to impose her capricious will on those around her all over again. That caused her to descend in the spiritual scale, although in human terms she seemed to "have ascended" socially.

When she resumed her existence as a spirit she was unhappy and disappointed in herself. She realized that it would have been better for her if the rich family had only made things easier for her and hadn't adopted her as a mere pawn in a chess game. To such people, anything that would make them win the game is a worthwhile move.

I am in favor that couples without children or even those who already have their own children or foster children opt for the adoption of abandoned children or orphans. In my long experience dealing with spirits I have been able to see that in order for a child to be adopted, often the way to arrive at a certain couple is through one of those births that seem "accidental."

One of my friends, an old man with adult children of his own, once found a crying infant on his front door. He took it in with all his love and is raising it devotedly in spite of all the sacrifices he and his wife have had to endure, now that they are finally free from the duty of bringing up their own children.

He told me that the boy, who is now a little older than three is the joy of their lives in spite of all the work and unpredictable situations that raising a child entails. Like me he believes that, in some mysterious way, this spirit was meant to belong to them and that they must be connected in some way.

Let me tell you one more story. The existence, later confirmed, of old connections between a girl, who was literally thrown into a couple's lap, and this couple.

Up to here, I have been sharing my own private opinions about the matters being discussed always *stressing* that they are not general rules. But now I shall mention an eternal and universal rule that will never fail: the law of love. If you love a child, take it in your arms and let that love inspire you. And even if it doesn't seem to be a wise decision for many reasons, go ahead and give it all the love in your heart. Your love can be very effective not in an exaggerated, possessive and selfish way. You can make that child's life easier. It is not your task to remove the obstacles she was programmed to overcome and to learn how to overcome. Do your best not to influence the free will of that child or of those around her. Give them the guidance you deem necessary, but leave the final decisions up to the child.

***

With these considerations we have somewhat anticipated our explanations.

Let's now go back, one step or two, because we haven't yet talked about what goes on in a spirit's mind in the dramatic moments when it is being reborn.

And that is what we shall learn in the next few pages.

Chapter 10.
WELL, LET'S GO!

The most dramatic testimonies collected by Dr.Helen Wambach are those reporting the emotions and perplexities involved in the moment someone is born, that is, the experience of coming into a new life. When diving into people's remote memories many unexpected details come up, some even paradoxical.

As seen before, the doctor managed to get memory reports from 84% of her universe of 750 patients, collecting very impressive accounts on the cosmic drama of birth. Studying some common points in the reports, the scientist was able to come to conclusions that revealed more than a few surprises. The first of these surprises was that dying is normally a pleasant experience, as it is a passage to freedom. It is the return to a dimension where people can have a much wider understanding about life. One can move at amazing speeds and understand things quickly. Being born implies uncertainty, worries, disquiet or plain disgust.

Many are not specific complaints from the unborn persons, but their considerations about critical or even negative situations they will encounter on the threshold of their new existence.

For the sake of brevity, let's try to shorten those statements.

Firstly let's speak about the physical act of birth. The baby comes from a stage in the maternal body, where it was enveloped in silence, warmth and darkness, a cozy and comfortable environment. As it comes out, many times in an abrupt, inadequate and violent manner, it is thrown into an extremely hostile world where three adverse factors come together to make it a terrible experience: the cold, intense light and noise. The reports are very similar as in most cases mothers give birth under the intense lights of the operating room, and for at least some moments the child is placed on a cold surface of a surgery room. The baby feels cold and abandoned while it hears the nervous movements and voices of the busy people around it. The noises of surgical and electrical equipment, especially when extraordinary procedures are called for to save the mother or the baby, all contribute to create a seemingly hostile environment. When the doctors try to rush the birth process a lot of suffering occurs because the baby doesn't usually feel ready to come to this side of life. It occurs in programmed deliveries and caesarian sections, procedures that are becoming progressively common, mostly for the convenience of doctors, or families, but not necessarily for the convenience of the child when choosing the time of its own birth. The sensation of being forced to be born before the right time is sometimes very intense as can be seen in the following account:

"As I was being born it seemed like something was trying to push me out. There was nothing I could do as there was nothing I could hold on to. Immediately after my birth I felt the unpleasant impact of cold air, shiny lights, and strangely dressed people."

Another person says: *"I felt very angry when I was born because I was being forced out before the right time. As soon as I was born I saw a very white wall right in front of me. I was not aware of the other people's feelings because I was too angry."*

I think that the point that must be stressed in such reports is the amazing sense of maturity, dignity, perception and sensitivity of the people that underwent regression. They went through the dramatic experience of being born not as an unconscious baby, who knows nothing, but as an experienced adult, aware of its personal traits and intellectual potential. Sometimes we can see a great intelligence and a wide and profound life experience in these people and besides, they have a lot of self criticism and are able to easily understand not only what is being said around them, but the thoughts and feelings of these people, even when their words don't match their feelings.

We have just mentioned how angry babies get by having to be born before they feel ready to do so. But there is much more to it. They clearly realize whether they are welcome and loved or whether they are rejected or treated with love, or whether they are rejected or treated as mere soulless individuals. The cold professional hastiness with which they are treated by doctors and nurses and the rejection or disappointment of parents, the jealousy of older siblings and the worries or irritation of grandparents are all very painful for these babies.. *"How can I possibly communicate with these people?"* A newborn asked himself. Another one said: *"It seemed to me that all the other people in the delivery room didn't understand what was going on and I knew everything. This seemed cosmically amusing......*

CHAPTER 10.

I felt that my spirit was looking at everything. I entered my body just before being born. What I saw after I was born was that the spanking the doctor gave me was quite unnecessary. I was furious. I knew the doctor had a terrible hangover."

"....it seemed to me that the doctors didn't realize I was a conscious human being and treated me as a non-being, a mere thing or object."

Look at this other statement:

'The experience on the way out was extremely vivid for me. I felt the warmth of the womb and the muscular contractions forcing me out. I felt like I was being pushed down when that intense light exploded in front of me, unpleasantly bright, making me wince. I could vaguely sense the thoughts and feelings of the doctors and nurses. It is not my present ego which accepted these ideas, for I thought that as a baby I was not supposed to be doing that. But the fact is that in a telepathic way I was becoming aware of their emotions."

Another person said that the people around were handling it without any love, "with great emotional indifference". And goes on to say:

"I was aware of their feelings. They were carrying out their jobs and meant well. But they were not aware of how cold they were, and how much I could tell what was going on."

One of the subjects understood that her parents were doing their best to accept her, making up for the reluctance they had to become parents, but the baby "knew the truth" even hearing them speaking about the future plans they had for her.

Another person says: "I had the intelligence of an adult."

"... a woman grabs me briskly. I feel she dislikes me. It seems that I have offended her in some way. My mother is too tired to show any feelings for me. The woman walks out of the room carrying me in her arms. I feel like a rejected criminal. True tears filled my eyes as she carried me away. In fact all I wanted was to return to the bright space where I had come from."

And this is not the only one who wished to return to the "place from where he had come", or to be more precise, the place which it wished it had never left..

Another one said: *"how stupid people are in not realizing what babies really want."*

"I was disappointed to find out that the joy I felt being born did not find an echo out here. I was aware and alert, but the people around me didn't know that."

"I didn't like the idea of being squeezed into that little body, but I agreed to do it and said to myself: OK, let´s go! And I jumped in as if I were diving into cold water."

"my mind was too developed for that little body."

"The doctor was too busy with his work, ignoring me as a human being."

"I felt like laughing at them, I don't know why. I guess it was because they didn't really know who I was, or what it meant to be born".

"My grandmother was really mean. In the beginning I thought she was a nurse, but soon I realized she was my grandmother."

There are many reports such as these, but if we mentioned all of them we would run the risk of sounding repetitive. I think, however, they were enough to convince us that instead of an "innocent" and dumb baby, incapable of thinking, feeling and understanding what goes on around it, what we have being born is a mature adult spirit with the rare capacity of perceiving subtle thoughts and feelings even before they are expressed.

Some important comments are in order.

Chapter 11.
MYSTERIES OF THE COMMUNICATION PROCESS

It seems obvious to admit that newborn babies do not understand the language spoken around them. But they don't have to, as they are able to understand thoughts and feelings that have not yet been put into words even when these words, thoughts and feelings do not correspond to the intimate truth of the person who expressed them.

Once, in a small study about animals, I wrote that I believe that in nature there's a kind of a primeval level of communication that is preexisting and doesn't require words, a kind of channel through which all living things – from plants to humans, including animals that we call irrational, can communicate. Therefore, communication would not rely on *words* but on the *feelings* that are behind them (or not).

If this weren't true, we wouldn't have so many clear and well documented evidence of communication between humans and animals or plants, or among plants and animals themselves.

The positive reactions of plants to good care, to soft talk, to the positive emotions of people taking care of them is now an accepted fact. The same happens with animals, and of course with people. It is not necessary for a person to talk in order for us to know if they are hostile towards us or if they like us. Sometimes it is possible to detect aggressiveness in smiles or nice words which are apparently friendly.

Emotions travel through this atavistic channel before they are put into words. Through this channel we can communicate with each other and with all living things within limitations. The small plant, for instance, cannot respond except by becoming stronger and producing better flowers and fruits. The puppy can do better: bark with joy and wag its little tail, turn its belly up, or run and hide in fear when scolded.

When I wrote a book about mediumship a spiritual friend told me that we have a mental circulation system he called *conductor* and another one used to express ourselves that he called *expresser*. The first is for mental communications that are not put into words. The translation of these thoughts into words takes place in the expresser system and we use it to communicate.(To communicate means to make common)

The famous scientist Lyall Watson reached a similar conclusion in his book *Supernature*:

"Physiologically we are not very different from other animals. Although we have an elaborate oral language system and other sophisticated means of communication, our bodies continue to express external signs of our deepest feelings."

In my opinion, however, the signs of this understanding do not manifest themselves as a bodily expression but as telepathy, a more subtle mechanism described by Dr. Wambach's patients.

This word, in spite of its more common meanings, fits well into this case. *Pathos* comes from Greek and usually means disease, illness, evil, but also passion, friendship, affection. This word describes certain types of *sensations* (being sick), or *emotions* (passion, affection, aversion). Therefore *telepathy* is a mechanism that transmits, at a distance, emotions that do not necessarily have to be expressed in words, as Watson correctly imagined.

Watson, whose writings I often read and admire wrote another book after *Supernature*, called *The Romeo Error* where he explains his ideas about the communication process among living things.

He examines the experiments of Clive Backster, who believes "all living things have a primary perception", and Watson elegantly calls this "the universal language of life".

Based on Backster's experiments, Watson was able to come to incredible conclusions. Let me describe his experiment with a girl named Tanya.

Tanya was hypnotized and asked to choose a number from 1 to 10 and not to tell him what number it was. Another person involved in the experiment began asking Tanya successively: "Is it number 1?" "No", she answered. "Is it 2?" "No". And so on, she denied all numbers from 1 to 10. But a plant, which took part in the experiment and was hooked up to a lie detector, gave in Tanya's secret revealing the chosen number had been 5. How else could the little plant reveal that secret, if not through the direct mechanism of the "universal language of life"?

Another one of Backster's experiments repeated and perfected by Watson, produced even more intriguing results. Backster took 18 eggs and placed them on a kind of small revolving table. Periodically, and randomly, one of the eggs rolled down from the table into a bowl of boiling water. Backster noticed that the egg hooked up to the detector showed an immediate reaction when his "companion" fell into the hot water, but showed no reaction when the same happened to any of the other 17 eggs, until at least 15 minutes had elapsed. What could explain this?

When he repeated the experiment, Watson found that the moment one of the eggs fell into the hot water bowl the other eggs became unconscious for fifteen minutes.

Watson concluded that the only possible explanation for this is that the egg which fell into the bowl sent off an alarm signal, and the other 17 eggs fainted from fear, and took about 15 minutes to recover consciousness.

Regarding the same subject, Watson mentions the traditions of the Sioux and other Native American Indians who follow rituals which we are only now beginning to understand. When it becomes necessary for the tribe to carve a new "totem pole", the tribe's elderly assemble and go into the woods in order to find a good tree for carving. Once that tree is found they all gather around it, and "talk" to it saying:

"Listen, tree, we are very sorry, but you know how important it is for us to have a "totem pole". The old one is falling apart so we need a new tree trunk and you have been chosen!"

As soon as they say this, they quickly go to the next tree and cut it down. According to Watson, no one has ever asked the Sioux why they perform such a strange ritual. But it's true that the wisdom of Indians is a fact. When these facts are put together with Backster's egg experiment, Watson is inclined to conclude that all the trees in the woods "faint" when the first one hears its death sentence. It is likely that the Indians choose to cut down an unconscious tree so that it will not suffer unnecessarily, although theirs is a noble cause.

The reader is naturally entitled to his own opinion. But I agree with Watson and he agrees with the Indians and the Indians are very wise when it comes to the secrets of nature.

Now let's return to Dr. Wambach.

I think that this form of wordless communication is a kind of communication that remains in the conductor channels my spiritual friend described and does not convert itself into any kind of symbol or code used in the expresser system. Even if it is only, as has been mentioned before, for internal use, the other living things in nature just happen to know what goes on inside other beings.

I am glad to observe that a patient of Dr. Wambach describes this phenomenon very clearly during her survey.

"After my birth I felt the presence of various sparse energies and intensities around me. I was able to feel what other people were feeling..." Things were completely obvious, but could not be explained or specified in an intellectual sense. (My italics).

All that was said above added to what remains in the obvious "non-intellectual" suggested by the Doctor's patient, leads us to an irrefutable truth: we can communicate with babies when they are born and even *before that*. They will not be able to answer in the way we expect adults to but their minds and hearts are open to feelings, emotions, conflicts, joy, affection or rejection as well as to all subtle thoughts we can imagine or not.

I said we can communicate with our babies, but let me add that we "should" do so. I cannot stress enough how important this is.

I have seen concrete examples of this, personal experiences and reports given by people very close to me who answered my questions on their experiences and observations.

One of these cases is briefly described in my book "Dialogue with Shadows".

We had worked for many months with a very difficult spirit who was still very hurt with one of the components of our group. It was a woman and they had lived in the last century when they had fallen madly in love and this relationship had left scars and negative consequences which lingered inside her. At the end of a long and careful conversation that went on for months, we were able to calm her spirit that at the time was preparing to be reborn. Such spirit would be born into the family of her former lover. This time she would be the daughter of a young woman who had been the couple's daughter in a former life. This would place her in the new life as her former lover's granddaughter.

The child was a few months old when I visited the family. The young mother invited me to see the baby who was sound asleep in its cradle. Afraid to wake her I asked the mother not to turn on the lights, but she insisted by saying that the child was used to having the light on and wouldn't wake up. In fact the baby remained asleep for some time while I looked at her silently feeling very emotional. Suddenly, she opened her tiny eyes and stared at me enigmatically, smiled and fell asleep again. It wasn't difficult to understand her wordless "message."

"Oh! Is that you? Here I am my friend."

There is another story worth telling.

I was once visiting the home of a family that had just adopted a baby girl a few months old when I was left alone with the baby for a brief moment. When I approached the little cradle- she was awake- and I started to talk softly to her saying that now she was safe. She had experienced worries and difficulty. She now had a home and nice people to take care of her. She could live peacefully. And I asked God to bless her soul.

Even though I was used to those things I was amazed at her unexpected reaction. She looked at me deeply with tears rolling down her face! It was obvious that she was trying hard to express the emotions in her heart. She wanted to tell me something so badly that her little face seemed very anxious. But there was not a trace of pain. All I could understand was the silent language of her tears, nothing else, but we were able to communicate at a level that requires no words.

I will speak about other such examples in the next chapter.

Chapter 12.
UNDERSTANDING THROUGH TALKING

A seven or eight year old boy was having problems at school, not as far as his studies were concerned but because he was taken by a strong sensation of panic, every time he entered the classroom. Sometimes he just could not stay. In other occasions he would ask his little sister to join him in class and to remain there till the end of the period, what was becoming a problem also for her. From the moment he started getting ready to school until when he returned home, it all became a problem for him and his family. They just didn't know anymore what to do.

They tried everything unsuccessfully. Was that child under the influence of troubled spirits? Did he just dislike the school? Did the parents need to be stricter and punish him? Did he have psychiatric problems?

A relative decided to tell spiritual friends about the boy's ordeal trying to get advice as to how the family should deal with the problem. The spiritual friends said that in a former existence in France the boy, at about the same age he was now, was attending school when a fire started and the classroom ceiling fell on the children. The boy had died then. This would be a typical example of a subconscious memory the boy had brought from a past existence, hence his inexplicable panic.

The spiritual friends told the family to treat the boy in a calm and understanding manner instead of resorting to physical punishments. They also told them to talk to the child every night in order to assure him that everything was well now, that they would protect him and nothing bad would happen at school.

That he should trust in God. Also they should explain the concept of reincarnation as his spirit was in condition to understand and accept what had happened to him as something natural. Finally, they should assure him that he was not under any negative influence but what was happening was exclusively his own problem.

CHAPTER 12.

The treatment worked.

In another family with very close ties to ours, a girl began displaying certain traits that were causing concern. As soon as she started talking and communicating with others her strong personality was evident and she was somewhat nervous and agitated. She showed no fear and was a little aggressive. Her sleep was restless and she always had terrible nightmares. Sometimes she pretended to be shooting at others with invisible guns as if she were in a battle. If she wanted a toy her elder sister was holding she would grab the toy and run away with it leaving her sister (a sweet little girl) in tears.

The girl´s health was not that good either. She would get sick often. Her stomach was frequently upset and didn't seem to react properly to the doctors prescriptions.

Another unexplained situation came along: she seemed to have problems with her feet which no clinical exams or X-rays seemed to identify. As soon as she started to talk, she would complain that her feet hurt even when she was asleep. Besides, she refused to wear shoes that had shoelaces. After a long time she finally accepted to wear a special kind of shoes which didn't seem to hurt her so much. When the shoes got old and had to be replaced a new problem started. She refused to wear any shoes that caused her the slightest discomfort. She wanted her feet always free as if she might need them for a sudden and vital escape.

Asked about this situation, the girl's parents spiritual friends explained that in her last life the girl had lived in France and was a "maquis", devoted by patriotic conviction to the famous underground organization that fought against the German occupation forces during World War II.

According to them, my dear little cousin had died tragically. The group she belonged to was crossing a mined field at night when her foot got caught in a briar patch. She asked her closest companion to help her but it was of no avail. As she couldn't free her foot an explosion shattered her body to pieces. She might have been able to escape the explosion, and save her life if her shoe hadn't gotten stuck.

They added that the damage caused to her physical body was so great that her perispiritual mold was of difficult recovery. So that she could reincarnate after remaining 40 years in the spiritual world, it had been necessary that a complex and delicate work of reconstitution took place

This way, upon returning, her physical body would not show deformities and mutilations. That was the reason for all her physical troubles which apparently had no real cause. She was obviously a gifted spirit, because if she weren't so she would not have deserved so much help and attention. As a result, she was sent to a couple with the best physical, intellectual and moral gifts. The spiritual friends further explained that in this particular case, a healthy physical body developed in adequate conditions would positively influence the spiritual body, helping it to recover.

With regard to the emotional aspects of this problem, the girl's mother was instructed to talk to her, especially when she was asleep, sending her messages that would calm her and convince her that her suffering was way behind her and were nothing more than bad memories. There were no wars to be fought at least not in that pacific region where she now lived, amid a loving and well balanced family. The mother should assure her over and over again that her feet were normal and perfectly healthy.

If the reader is up to it, I have one more story which illustrates the extraordinary maturity of a young mother just past her teenage years. Because this case has serious connotations it requires a special chapter where it can be further discussed.

But before that, I have a personal story to tell.

I was never an agitated or troublesome boy. Much to the contrary, I was usually shy and quiet. Once, when I was about seven or eight years old, I unexpectedly did "something" that could have had tragic consequences.

We lived near the railroad. I was born quite close to the tracks. A train was passing and I decided to test my strength and target by throwing a rock at it. The stone I had thrown at the train, which happened to be a passenger train, broke one of its windows. Fortunately no one was hurt.

But from the next station they called the station near my house, and it was not hard to find out who was to blame for the "terrorist" act.

I don't recall if my parents spanked me (they usually didn't) but I

CHAPTER 12.

remember they grounded me and made me to sit on a pile of logs near the tracks where everyone could see me. Besides feeling humiliated, I could not understand the reasons for all that commotion. After all, "all" I had done was throw a rock at the train.

Sometime later a young man who worked for my father at the station came and started talking to me. His name was David, Theobaldo David Silva, and even now, 60 years after that day, I remember that his birthday was on January,1. It is a coincidence that I am writing these lines on December 31, and that in a few hours my friend David, who is probably no longer here with us, would be celebrating his birthday. I will always be grateful to him for his words to me on that day.

He wasn't there to censor me nor did he criticize my father's strict punishment. All he did was to explain things to me in an adult way. I don't remember his exact words but he explained that my irresponsible act might have hurt or even killed someone on the train. People shouldn't do things like that. To sum it up, he appealed to my dignity, which was at the time very low as I sat on the pile of logs. He helped me develop a sense of responsibility.

I remember the strong impact his words had on me. I really had not thought about the possible consequences of my thoughtless act. What if my irresponsible gesture had blinded or even killed someone?

I think David realized how important his words were to me, as they were both useful and understanding. And although it was never revealed to me, I think David convinced my father to release me from my punishment.

Never again did I throw stones at anybody, although many times in my life rocks were thrown at me. But who hasn't been hit by rocks? As I like to say, we have more to learn from mistakes than from good behavior, and David's lesson became permanently engraved in my mind. May God keep him in peace wherever he may be today. I believe that he was one of the first people in my life that talked to me like an adult instead of censoring, reprimanding and criticizing me. He didn't use irony or aggressiveness. Above everything, he *explained* the situation.

I would find myself in similar situations other times in my life. Before any condemnation or hasty criticism, it was always my desire that someone would tell me in a calm and polite way, where, when and why I had gone wrong. They could condemn me later, I would accept it, but what I wanted was to understand the causes of my behavior, so that I could avoid making the same mistakes again. Once having understood what had been done wrong, the shame of having done it would be punishment enough. That is why I never considered punishments necessary. Spanking, reprimanding and punishing I thought were worthless and therefore unnecessary acts.

This book was already being written when a lady friend told me a similar story. In a moment of impatience and irritation she lost control and began shouting at her young son. The boy, very calmly addressed her in more or less the following words:

"Mummy, don't talk to me like that! You know how an upset person feels like for I have seen you cry when this happens to you."

The woman came to her senses. She had received a lesson from the one *she* was supposed to teach. She smiled, hugged the boy, and when she calmed down said:

"You're right son! You're a very nice boy!"

If there is a lesson to be learned from this chapter it would be this: talk to your son or daughter no matter how old they are. As popular wisdom has it: "by talking one shall understand one another…" And what can be more necessary and urgent in this chaotic world than understanding among people?

Here is a special piece of advice to pregnant women: talk to the "person" inside your womb. Tell the baby you love it, that you are waiting for it with an open heart and that it may count on you for whatever is possible. Use your hands to softly caress the baby. The magnetism of love is easily transmitted in the form of positive energy flowing from the fingers.

Chapter 13.
A YOUNG MOTHER'S EXPERIENCE AND OBSERVATIONS

In this chapter I will show you an example of an excellent mother and child relationship. I asked her to describe her experiences and observations in writing so that I could include them in this book. I liked what she wrote so much I decided to reproduce the exact words she used to show the emotional charge of her words.

Here is her story:

"Rafael is a very sweet and calm baby. The first time I talked to him was in an elevator on my way down from the laboratory where I had just found out I was pregnant. I told him that I had started loving him at that very moment, and that he would be very welcome. I went on to say that he had to prepare himself to come to a world that wasn't so good but that he could count on me for anything he needed from that day on.

"From that day on we started talking about everything. I wanted to give him a clear picture of what to expect here on Earth. Sometimes I feel I am quite small, like a student trying to teach basic things to a super-intelligent professor. But I go on, anyway, for I'm sure that he will have all my love in his heart as I try to tell him about the things on our Earth.

"As an example of what I have said above, I will mention a conversation we had on Christmas Eve, while I was writing out Christmas cards. I told him, as if I were talking to an adult that we were approaching the date when men celebrate the birth of Christ but that unfortunately many of these men had no idea what they were celebrating. These people, I told Rafael, invented Santa Claus, a mythical figure people talked about and celebrated during Christmas with much food and drink. But I also explained to him that this childish legend is aimed at boosting sales in December, with people buying Christmas gifts in stores, which enjoy the best profit this time of the year.

And this is what I did with almost everything else. I try to talk to him all the time showing him that on Earth we are all very selfish and not very honest or civilized, but that we should look for existing good qualities in everything and everyone. That's what's really important.

While Rafael was growing inside me, my mother and I tried to avoid spending too much on his baby trousseau, but the handmade pieces were important specially because of the love and care they transmit to whom we offer them. I often told Rafael about the love I put into my work dedicated to him and tried to have him participate in my daily chores.

In our family prayers I always repeated welcoming words of love to him. In two of these moments of prayer I had the exact sensation that he was sitting next to me with his hand resting on my shoulder. It was quite difficult to imagine that little baby being formed inside me to be that adult spirit!

"We always talked about the development of his little body. Each new week along the pregnancy was studied and read about by the two of us with much attention. We both followed the formation of every organ or external part of Rafael's little body, now comfortably nested in my arms. This is quite marvelous!

"I would like to mention some facts as they were quite interesting. I cannot state, however, if they were mere coincidences.

"Before Rafael was born I told him many times that we didn't own a home of our own, that we had to live with other people that probably would not appreciate hearing a baby crying too much and that I had had the disturbing experience of hearing a baby crying all day and also all night. I told him that he should be a nice baby, and shouldn't cry so much, especially at night.

"And so Rafael was born a very, very nice baby. It is even possible to say that he has never woken anyone up with his crying. He hardly ever cries which is a mystery to those who meet him.

"Another fact worth mentioning is what happened when he was one month old and I was sick with the flu and had a very bad sore throat. Up to then Rafael had seldom slept through the night alone in his crib, as he usually sleeps with me until today. When I put him in his cradle he would start complaining until I placed him beside me in my bed. Even when he is sound asleep he shows me he knows it when I put him down in his crib. But, as I didn't want him to catch

CHAPTER 13.

my cold I explained to him that he would have to spend all night in his crib because I had a fever and didn't want him to get sick.

"My sweet baby slept alone that whole night, and then for another two nights, without complaining, until I got better and he could sleep with me again. On his first night alone he didn't complain at all.

"A few days later, another fact worth mentioning happened just before he was two months old, when my mother left me alone with him for the first time. I have to confess that I was somewhat confused in dealing with everything. I had a lot of ironing to do that day and Rafael was a little cranky and wanted me to hold him. I asked him to nap for a couple of hours so that I could finish ironing, take a bath and go to bed. It was late, and I asked him to sleep until 6 PM. He not only slept until the time I asked him to but also, after waking up, waited quietly for me while I showered and we could go to sleep.

"Another interesting event happened on December 24, when we were staying at my in-laws. My mother-in-law asked me to help her wrap some Christmas gifts. There were a lot of them and we didn't have much time, just the rest of that morning and the following afternoon. I put Rafael on my in-laws' bed, showed him all the gifts I had to wrap, and told him how important it was to get it done by the end of the afternoon. I asked him to help me by not requesting my attention a lot. Rafael remained very quiet lying in bed, and eventually fell asleep which seldom happens unless he is in my lap. He slept for a long time despite the noise the wrapping paper made. When he finally woke up he remained calm and quiet until I had finished my work."

"These are the most interesting facts I have registered. When I remember them a doubt comes to my mind: were they mere coincidences or does Rafael really understand me?

Today I feel I am not sure enough to confirm it. I also feel that with each passing day Rafael is more like a child. It seems that over time he is slowly losing the ability he had of understanding me."

"Rafael was three months old on January 22.

"January, 1986.

"Alda"

***

This excellent report is a testimony of love in its purest form. But there's much more to it. It shows a feeling of deep respect, almost reverence, from a mother to a son from the moment she welcomed him into the world and assured him of her dedicated support as soon as she knew she was pregnant. A true example of humbleness is given by this young mother when she candidly confesses feeling "somewhat small" when she tried to explain to an experienced being how things were on Earth. She seemed to know he already knew everything there was to know and that her explanation would just be another way of showing him how much she cared, in the same way the little clothes she had made for him showed how much she loved him.

Another point worth mentioning is the presence she felt next to her of a reincarnating spirit, mature and adult, who put a hand on her shoulder at the holy moment of a prayer, while the baby was still growing inside her.

Alda teaches us another important lesson when she says that with every passing day she felt that Rafael "was becoming more like a child" and was slowly losing his ability to understand her.

This is an important truth that would have escaped me if Alda hadn't mentioned it.

Let's examine it more carefully:

When comparing Dr. Wambach's experiments to the teachings transmitted to Allan Kardec by the instructors in his Codification (see chapter VII- Return to Bodily Life- of the "Book of Spirits"), we can come to the following general conclusions:

1) The process of reincarnation is a much more disturbing and above all "a much longer" process for the spirit than the process of dying. " In death" - as described in question number 339 – " the spirit is free whereas when it is born it becomes a prisoner. Its situation is similar to that of "an adventurer setting out to sea and risking his life in the rough waves as "the trials and tribulations of his life will make him progress or fall behind according to how well he has faced them"

2) Because human beings have a long childhood, the spirit spends this time more *linked* to the body than really *incarnated in* it.

3) The spirit does not identify itself with matter. It only takes on some of its properties. Matter is only the form the spirit needs to act in the world. "When united to a body the spirit maintains all the qualities of its spiritual nature."

4) The spirit in a child's body can be as mature and developed as that of an adult's, or even more so, if it happens to be more evolved, "for what keeps it from manifesting its true potential is the incomplete development of its human organs. It will act according to the possibilities of the new body."

5) Childhood is considered by the instructors as "a resting period for the spirit".

6) "When reincarnated for the purpose of perfecting itself, the spirit is during childhood, more open to impressions that will help its development. It is then that those in charge of helping in its education will have a better chance of changing its personal traits and curb its negative tendencies. This is the role God reserved to parents, a sacred mission they should strive to accomplish."

There is, therefore, a period in which the spirit is more attached to the body than properly incarnated in it. During this period the spirit will have relative freedom. As long as this period lasts, the spirit will be able to perceive what goes on around it and even know what people are thinking. But as its physical body develops and its organs mature it becomes integrated to the world around it. At this point its spiritual abilities start to dwindle and it becomes increasingly limited due to the biological boundaries of its body. This body will then be guided by this spirit in the difficult task of living on Earth. As a result of this, the spirit loses its full capacity to use the purely spiritual faculties that it had in its former state of spiritual freedom. From that moment on it will act in life as an incarnated being who is confined to the limits of a physical body. It will no longer be able to grasp the thoughts and emotions of other people, and will only understand what is said in a language that he is starting to learn. On the other hand, it will increasingly learn to manifest its emotions and reactions, in spite of its still limited vocabulary.

From then on, only when asleep will the spirit enjoy some freedom as at that time it will be partially disconnected from the physical body. According to the spiritual instructors this is the best moment to talk directly to the spirit as we have seen before, in some specific cases.

Alda's impressions were therefore correct, as she noted that "as times goes by Raphael is becoming much more of a boy", and is progressively losing the capacity to understand her through the channels that Lyal Watson elegantly calls "the universal language of life", and is starting to communicate in the language spoken by the people in whose community he was reborn. This is why the instructors briefly stated that "in death the spirit becomes free, in birth it becomes a slave". And that is why Dr. Wambach's regression patients reported they find it wonderful to die but full of tensions the act of being born. Once caught in its little cage, and within closed doors, the spirit ends up forgetting the amount of space it had before being reborn.

Dying is like "going back home", to where we came from before we were reborn.. But wait! Death is only liberating when it happens at the right time, when the spirit has completed its mission on Earth with dignity, and has lived in accordance with divine laws. Those who are rebellious, violent, and suicidal will not be free; they will only change prisons, up until they are corrected. That is the law...!

Chapter 14.
WE ONLY FORGET WHAT WE KNOW

The reader not used to the reality of reincarnation may very well think: "Good, but if I have lived other lives, why can't I remember them?"

This is a legitimate question and deserves a legitimate answer. In fact, we usually *don't remember* our former lives but this doesn't mean we *haven't lived* before. You can forget a birthday gift you got five or six years ago. Nevertheless, the gift, if it lasts, is probably still there, forgotten in a drawer or a closet.

And it's a good thing we forget so that we can use the chance of starting a new life in a better way as if we were starting with a clean slate to write the story of our life.

It's a good thing not to remember that in past lives you had serious problems with the person who now is your mother, brother or a difficult sister. It isn't easy to know that you have brutally deceived the beautiful girl that is now your daughter, or that you have stolen the inheritance that in fact belonged to that son-in law that you didn't want your daughter to marry.

Families are often arrangements made in the invisible world involving the characters of former dramas or tragedies. They are joined together so that they can settle old disputes or grievances through the general rules of brotherly love and try to be happy together some time in the future. Our former victims and enemies, the people we have hurt, those who meant to do us harm when it could be avoided had we all acted righteously, may all be born around or close to us. But of course, according to our merits, wonderful people we love and respect are born around us too, but this is almost an exception, not a rule. Didn't the Christ say that we should make peace with our enemies?

He also said that we would not be free from suffering, until we paid all our debts to the laws of love. And that the one who makes a mistake, becomes a slave to that mistake. Do you remember his few, albeit love-filled, words: "Go and do not sin again so that nothing bad may happen to you"? Well, that's it!

So the family is the testing field, where we will encounter friends and foes. The former will bring us the pleasant warmth of their affection, in an easygoing and constructive relationship. It is very easy to love them. It will not be easy to love the latter as they unconsciously keep unsolved hostilities towards us, pains that can't yet be overcome. It is much more difficult to love them, and to make their negativity become a true loving relationship. But let us as again cite Christ who knew everything, saw everything and advised all:

"Love your enemies" Luke 6:27, *"Do good to those who hate you, bless those who curse you, pray for those who abuse you"*. And further on 6:32 *"If you love those who love you what benefit is that to you? For even sinners love those who love them"*.

This philosophy which seems so strange has deep motivations. There are no problems to be settled with those we love. They are already our friends and treating them with affection and respect will be enough. But we have unsettled matters with those who hate us, even when we are not consciously aware of them. For some hidden reason we are placed together to practice brotherly love. And here again we should remember the wise words of Christ:

"Make peace with your enemy while you are still with him on the way".

These are wise words. He is on the way with us precisely because we have to make peace with him and make him our friend instead of our enemy. This will be an easier task if we don't know the reasons behind our difficulties. But on the other hand, the value of the reconciliation work will be greater if it is performed as a true effort to gain the trust and brotherly love of the one who does not love us and not as an obligation of making amends with a former enemy.

Moreover, you will not be doing this to a stranger or an unknown person, but to a son, a father, a mother or a brother. You will be doing it to someone who is very close to you.

Something else to know is that it's better for us not to remember everything, because when the weight of guilt gets too heavy, remorse may threaten to overcome us and paralyze the reparation process. You may think it would be better to know everything from the start,

CHAPTER 14.

but that is not always true. In our ignorance we are protected from certain regrets and embarrassments. This is so true that we often choose to forget the silly acts of when we were young and hadn't yet reached the serenity of adulthood.

A short while ago I told you about what happened to me when I was around eight years old, and threw a rock at a passing train. You know what? It was hard for me to put this incident down on paper, to write about it. It wasn't easy, but what made me decide was the conviction that the episode could be a useful lesson for my readers as it had been for me. At that moment I learned the lesson about personal responsibility. But between us, I'd rather have left this incident locked in one of the secret drawers of my mind. Or better still, I wish it had never happened at all. Can you imagine if instead of throwing a rock at a passing train you had beheaded or poisoned a girl that is now your own favorite daughter? A girl that doesn't care much for you, and still doesn't trust you?(I recommend you read the true story "The Sad Bleat of the Lost Sheep" in my book "The Exiled".)

Well, here are some of the main reasons we forget about our past lives. We must forget in order to make a fresh start in a new life, as if nothing had happened. It happens, though, that old memories and experiences from former lives can overflow from one life to another, as we have seen in cases mentioned in this book.

These memories are not always clear. They appear under different disguises, for instance, when you feel an immediate attraction or an extreme aversion toward someone you have just met. There are people we like from the start, whom we trust and feel perfectly at ease with, as there are those that no matter how hard they try to be nice to us we only accept with great reluctance.

I like to tell little stories to exemplify situations. These are absolutely authentic stories with no traces of fiction. I have told the following story before, in one of my books.

It is the story of an intelligent and well educated lady that called me to talk about some of her personal problems. What she really wanted was to undergo hypnosis, performed by me or by a specialist recommended by me so that she could understand why she couldn't stand her mother.

She said her mother was affectionate, dedicated and very friendly, always trying to be nice and pleasant, but she could not help feeling uneasy around her and even finding her repulsive. She avoided eating food her mother brought to her and had to wash her hands after she left. Naturally, it was very hard for her to deal with this repulsion. After all it was her own mother who was trying very hard to please her and had no idea of her daughter's feelings towards her.

This was her problem. And she thought regression therapy would enable her to overcome this painful situation and if it was impossible to love her mother at least she could learn to overcome her aversion and mistrust.

Then it was my turn to give her my opinion on the problem.

I said I wouldn't recommend a regression, even if it would be possible for me to do it, because that was not my purpose since my experiences in this field were limited to gathering information for my book *"Memory and Time"*.

It wouldn't be advisable for her because she could be faced with an extremely painful and traumatic episode that would worsen the situation instead of easing her pain. Besides, I didn't find it necessary for a simple and logical reason. It was not difficult to imagine the source of the whole problem between her and her mother. It must have been a serious offense committed by her mother against her, in a previous life. I had no idea what the offensive behavior was, but I could imagine that it might even be something very serious such as poisoning.

Maybe her mother had tried to poison her in another life. This would explain why she hated her mother's cooking. Her suffering couldn't be denied and it was clear that her mother might even have killed her in another life.

Anyway all that belonged to the past. They were matters that should have been forgotten. But distrust, fears and bad feelings remained. In spite of this, I made her understand that her mother was trying very hard to settle things, to make up for the mistakes and offenses she had made, to redeem herself from her evil doings. To my understanding she should try to make an effort to accept her mother who was certainly no longer the same person she had been.

The young lady listened to my words and seemed to meditate for a while. It felt like something was happening inside her. She took a deep breath, as if she were relieved, thanked me, and said she felt

CHAPTER 14.

ready to reconsider everything and strive to forge a new relationship with her mother. And this was exactly what I had asked God for both of them. I told the young lady to contact me again if she needed to but as I never heard from her again I can easily conclude that there was no longer a serious tension between daughter and mother.

In this case we didn't need to dive deeply into the emotional molds of these two lives but it was easy to imagine that there had been serious conflicts in a former existence.

There are, however, cases of children and adults who are able to accurately remember important parts of their previous lives and some who are able to remember their whole previous life and are even able to identify their enemies, friends or relatives. And at this point it is important to stress that people are joined together for a reason and not as a result of chance.

It would be indiscreet of me to do so, but I could easily write a small book about myself and my relatives containing details about our past lives together. This is a very delicate matter that touches sensitive points in most people. Spiritual friends of mine once told me that I had been prepared to know some, maybe many, episodes of my former lives, because of the role I am expected to play in this present existence. But I am not sure however, if those who share blood ties, work ties and affection ties with me, would have been equally prepared to absorb the impact of certain facts that may cause very stirring intimate conflicts

In Dr. Wambach's regression surveys and also in the work of the not less competent Dr.Edith Fiore we can see that the patient must undergo a preliminary test which shows if he is prepared to deal with traumatic events from the past which might be potentially explosive in the present. Sometimes the procedures have to be postponed or even cancelled, in order to stop the patient from getting even more troubled than he already is.

That reminds me of a man trying to get rid of his feelings of claustrophobia. He was deeply disappointed in himself after learning that in a former existence he had been a pirate of the kind who used to rob ships loaded with treasures at high seas, and then hide the treasures in a secret island. His goal was to "retire" from his criminal activities, and then enjoy a calm and respectable life.

In one of his trips to the island where he had gone to hide the latest treasures he had stolen, he was inside a tunnel dug in the ground and the earth collapsed, killing him just before he could reach the useless treasure.

In this case too, the memories of this event remained in his subconscious, and were not completely erased. They gave him a clear warning sign which could be felt as an unexplainable and overwhelming sensation of claustrophobia.

It should be stressed again that in some people, especially children, these memories are impressively real. It is advisable that you, as a parent, know how to deal with such problems when they affect your children.

And that is what we'll be talking about in the next chapter.

Chapter 15.
PEOPLE WHO CAN REMEMBER PAST LIVES

Out of the six hundred children surveyed by Dr. Ian Stevenson for his book published in 1966, *Twenty Cases Suggestive of Reincarnation*, only twenty were able to spontaneously remember their past lives. This was enough to make the famous scientist conclude that there was solid evidence to prove that reincarnation really existed.

Dr. Stevenson, with whom I had the honor of keeping in touch with by mail, is an internationally renowned scientist who held the important position of Director of the Department of Psychiatry in the University of Virginia, USA. He faced resistance and hostility when, as an open minded and modern scientist, he embraced the theory of reincarnation. He was a pioneer, and without a doubt, contributed much to the fact that today, after nearly 30 years, the reality of reincarnation is beginning to be discussed, studied, and finally accepted, after many other studies, documents and reports, including personal testimonies were made public. This entire movement was triggered by Dr. Stevenson's initial interest in the subject.

Dr. Stevenson carried out a careful investigation using all the necessary preliminary procedures required from a scientist to prove his point. He was from the start openly inclined towards accepting reincarnation after having compared it to various other alternatives worth examining. With time his position on the subject became even more solid, a fact demonstrated by his followers.

It is important to remember that a specific fact led Dr. Stevenson to believe something he only imagined to be true. This fact was the presence of birth marks that some children are born with, which are the result of wounds they suffered in former lives, and therefore *in other physical bodies.*

In chapter 3 (page 340) of his above mentioned book published in 1966, Dr. Stevenson writes: "I would like to call the reader's attention to a special kind of evidence (birth marks and deformities) that cannot be explained by extra-sensorial perception, and that can only be explained by influences on the physical body that occur prior to birth.

It is possible that my readers may have a child in their families, who is able to remember one or more of their former existences. Such spontaneous memories are more common than we imagine, and they are not normally detected because the people around the child, who are ignorant as to their meaning, will think they are the product of the child's vivid imagination.

It would be amazing if, after so many years dealing with spiritual reality, I would not have had the chance of witnessing some of these cases.

We have recently mentioned that, in spite of the fact that children are not able to remember previous lives, some will present symptoms or behaviors that are later identified as consequences of a situation they had gone through in past incarnations. In the case of my dear little cousin who had been a "maquis" in a previous life in France during World War II, it was not possible so far to define her former personality, and it is quite possible that we will never be able to do so, unless we are helped by complex accidental "coincidences". But that's not important.

The case of the boy told by Dr. Jorge Andrea isn't based on spontaneous memories. either. I know, however, that the child's development could be foreseen, and it cannot be questioned that he has the same personality traits he had in his former life. I don't know up to what point Dr. Andrea intends to or if he could or should follow through with his investigations or reports on this case, but I am quite sure that it would be extremely interesting from a historical, human and scientific perspective to share this with the public, provided the boy isn't hurt by it.

A personal report made directly to me by an adult, allowed me to obtain a great deal of information that is pertinent to this type of study.

The woman who talked to me was able, from early childhood, to remember the most important aspects of not only one but many of her lives. Besides, she was able to notice the subtle successive mechanism that makes lives fit into each other, with perfect precision like the parts in a puzzle, in accordance with logical, intelligent

CHAPTER 15.

planning and clearly verifiable objectives.

Some of the material supplied by this lady was used in two of my previously published books (*Spiritism and Human Problems* and *The Exiled*), and it would be irrelevant to talk about them again here, even if we were to focus on different aspects or details. I would like to mention a good example of how lives fit into each other which is an important part of her testimonial.

In one of her previous lives she held a high and powerful position of command and allowed or determined that a few people would be put to death due to political reasons. Three or four lives later she suffered from an incurable genetic disease that came as part of a redemption plan thought out by divine laws. As her former decisions against the sacrificed people had resulted in bloody acts, where else could her penance come from but from her own blood? And this is what happened. At a certain point along a life that was not easy, in an existence marked by extreme poverty, anguish, humiliation, deprivation and more than a few achievements in spite of all her problems, the young lady found out she suffered from sickle-cell anemia. No other disease would have been more appropriate to teach someone about the importance of blood to a human being. The life of a person suffering from that disease is a constant struggle against the insufficient red blood cells needed to supply vital oxygen to different parts of the body.

In another case involving spontaneous memories from previous lives, a man whom we will call André, was unexpectedly involved. He had just been introduced to a very nice lady and her seven-year-old granddaughter, whom we will call Renata. Andre addressed the little girl with tender words and bent down to kiss her face.

There was no time to start a conversation, as he would have an appointment in a few minutes. They waved each other goodbye and went off in different directions. A few days later André called to know about his new little friend, whom as he later found out, was an old acquaintance from many, many centuries before in a life in which they had had a lasting, pure and loving relationship. The apparently accidental meeting caused a considerable emotional impact on both of them, and seemed to have unleashed Renata's personal memories from her past. Not being able to know how or why, she began talking about facts from André's life she could not have known under normal circumstances. It was not her imagination. She simply *knew* about events and situations with absolute precision. Furthermore, she seemed to know, with great certainty, about her friend's psychological and personality traits.

The girl was not connected to André in this present life but she told him about her former life in a natural and spontaneous way. Now she is living in harmony, in a well balanced home with loving parents who have a stable economic situation but she describes a former existence of want and discomfort, when she lacked adequate clothing and housing. She recalls that her "former mother" could not even bake her a birthday cake. But she doesn't seem to have any hard feelings towards this period of poverty and suffering and also, paradoxically, no special enthusiasm for her present life. She seems to be the kind of person who would have preferred to stay where she was before.

Once she told her mother: "I didn't want to be born!"

"But, why not?" asked the mother.

"Because I didn't want to go through everything again!" she replied.

"But you seem so happy! You wake up smiling every day..." said the mother.

"Oh, but now that I was born again, there's nothing I can do about it", replied the little girl.

It's important to say that there were serious complications during her birth that put her life in danger, and obviously that of her mother's. The fact that these many difficulties were overcome reveals the possibility of calling it a miracle, if this word weren't so misused.

Renata first mentioned a previous life - spontaneously like all the other times- when she was between three and four years old. She said her name was Shi-Ni-Nin, and that she was Chinese or Japanese (she could not distinguish between these two nationalities). She said she had been a dancer, and reproduced some of the gestures and body expressions that are typical of oriental dances. The taste for Chinese objects remains in this life.

But it was only after she met André that she began to talk often and in great detail about memories from former lives that were awakened by common incidents of her normal daily routine. The

CHAPTER 15.

mother never started or forced this process, but listened to her stories in a very interested and emotional way, of course. Her interferences were limited to simple questions that would allow the girl to organize the story in a better way.

Let us address the following examples:

1) When her father refused to buy her a toy refrigerator (the kind that comes with miniature kitchens), she complained to her mother who diplomatically replied:

"Renata, your father isn't rich and can't give you everything you want."

And she answered in the affirmative and straightforward manner she usually did:

"That's not true! To begin with, I don't want *everything*!" (And that is true, she is not demanding and is content with little, she has a good idea of money's worth). "Besides, it isn't true that he is that poor. My former father had to borrow money to fix the roof of our house as he had none. But my father now, remodeled this whole apartment because it was so old and ugly and never asked for a penny. Is that being poor? And when I ask for a toy refrigerator he says he has no money..."

"Well" – her mother asked – "but are you happy with your present father?"

"No", answered the girl, but after a little while she added: "Yes, I do love my father Zé Carlos, I do!"

2) In another deeply emotional time the family was spending their vacation at a beach house. There were 6 people there: Renata, her mother, her brother, an aunt and two cousins. Renata insisted on going for a dive in the ocean that was very rough that morning. She swam for a while and stayed in the water for a long time. Although the sea was rough she wasn't afraid at all.

It is her mother who gets nervous with her courage. Renata seems to think of the ocean as being friendly, and not a powerful and fearful monster.

"But my dear", said the mother when she refused to get out of the water, "the sea is very rough today. It's very dangerous!"

"I'll be careful!" she answered.

"The sea is rough and you know I'm so scared. What if you drown? What am I going to tell your father?" asked the mother.

"Oh! Is that what's bothering you? Well, don't be afraid, I have drowned before and it won't happen again!"

Aunt and mother exchanged intrigued looks.

"You drowned?" asks the mother, "What do you mean you drowned?"

And this is what prompted the girl to start telling parts of a story about a dramatic existence; a poor, cumbersome and, to our knowledge, short life.

She had lived with her family: father, mother and two siblings- in a kind of a shack near the ocean. The father supported the family with odd jobs. They would eventually eat fish that was given to them by generous fishermen. The mother was a beggar and Renata helped her. Were they ashamed to beg? Of course not! They were very poor and there was no other way they could get the money they needed to survive! The shack they lived in had a straw roof. They only bathed in the ocean (that was why she was so familiar with it), but as they didn't have appropriate swimsuits, she explained, using mimic, she rolled her dress up to her neck and went into the water in her underwear. And as they had no towels, they had to wait for their bodies and clothes to dry off.

On that tragic day she had had a fight (not described) with an old man, their next door neighbor. She was very upset and told her mother she would go for a swim in the ocean. She was so upset she didn't notice that she had gone in too deep. A strong wave hit her and she drowned. The beach was deserted at the time. There was only a boat in the distance, and no one could hear her cries for help.

At this moment in Renata's report there was a deep emotional silence, as all of those listening were overwhelmed by the dramatic atmosphere that prevailed. After a few moments Renata's brother in her present life asked her whether she had had siblings in her former life. She said she had had two: a sister who was 3 years old and a brother who was 10. Her name was Bibi and her brother's was Guilherme. She couldn't remember her little sister's name. Had it all happened in Brazil? Probably not, as Guilherme is a common name

CHAPTER 15.

in many different languages: William in English, Wilhelm in German, Guillaume in French, Guglielmo in Italian, etc.).

In order to get her to go on talking the mother asked:

"What about your friend André? Is he in this story?"

Although she was still involved in her distant memories, Renata's face lit up with an affectionate expression as she said that André was a very kind man who lived nearby and gave her clothes, toys, candy, shoes and everything else she needed. He also used to help her mother by giving her some money.

When asked at what age she had died, she kept a distant and vague look and wrote the number 12 on the sand, writing the number 1 upside down. Going back in time to when she had been a poor illiterate beggar, she seemed to write the numbers with her former memory, but with the knowledge she had acquired in the present life, as she was just beginning to learn letters and numbers. There are quite a few examples of how lives fit into each other like a puzzle.

The importance of her report is not limited to its dramatic content, but to the way it discloses her convictions, to the way she faces death as a natural, certain and real mechanism that allows life to renew itself.

Once, when watching a movie on TV in which one of the characters seemed desperate in the face of death, Renata said: "I don't see what all the fuss is about! Dying is nothing. I have died many times, and as I can remember this is the fourth time I am returning..."

In another incident, after a day Renata had helped her mother more than usual, because the maid hadn't come, her mother kissed her and said: "Oh, what a nice and sweet daughter you are! Sometimes it's too good to be true to know that you are really my daughter, that I have such a wonderful daughter!"

Renata answered: "You can be sure of that! I was a spirit and then I got into your belly, and now I am your daughter!"

As can be seen, Renata is a mature spirit who brought a solid set of convictions to her new life. And this is revealed by her great ability to analyze all the situations in life and in the way she expresses her ideas. Despite her present biological immaturity, she shows she has acquired a vast experience in her former lives.

Although she refers to memories of only four of these lives, it is not difficult to presume that we are facing a soul with an impressive potential and a kind of authority that is the consequence of authentic wisdom. We would soon have an unexpected demonstration of that.

A certain rebellious and difficult spirit we were working with at our group, came to us one night as if he had no other choice or excuse not to seek our help. Renata had *demanded* that he come see us. The emotional connection that joins an unknown past and the present is the only hope he had of redemption as he had made many mistakes in his former lives.

Please note how Renata sounds true in the words in the following paragraph:

After she talked about her difficult previous life in which she had drowned, her present mother touched by the girl's sad testimony, asked her:

"Renata, why do you remember such difficult moments?"

"I don't know, mummy... I don't know why I remember them..." she answered.

And her mother insisted:

"Everyone likes to remember the pleasant moments in their lives but you only remember the bad ones, why is that?"

"Because they are true." said Renata with a disconcerting and logical simplicity, "If I were to lie I wouldn't remember."

Children are very wise and they try to pass this wisdom to us, but we don't often pay attention to them. In my book *Memory and Time* I have adopted the best definition I could find to describe the mysteries of memory:

"Memory", an anonymous child said, 'is what we use to forget".

And isn't this true? We can only forget what we once knew, or as Renata said, what one day was a reality in our lives.

***

The memories of isolated or sequential episodes of one or more lives can acquire different forms: rapid flashes of clairvoyance, under the disguise of dreams or similar dreamy states, or various incidents

CHAPTER 15.

in the present life that are symmetric or similar to facts from our past lives. In my opinion, however, they are more often brought back by encounters in this life with people whom, in one way or the other, were linked to us in former lives, either in good or bad times.

Specialized literature has well-documented cases in which the reincarnations were previously planned and carried out. Two of these cases happened in Brazil, in the family of the well-known Professor Francisco Waldomiro Lorenz and were included in the above mentioned book written by Dr. Ian Stevenson. In one of these cases the person was still alive when he himself announced his future reincarnation in the Lorenz family, and this really happened, as it could later be verified by many irrefutable evidences that resulted from the studies performed by Dr. Stevenson. In the case I have mentioned before regarding the baby girl who woke up to greet me with a beautiful smile, she had no recollections from her past life. But, people who met her while she was still in the spiritual world had no difficulties in identifying her in a previous life in nineteenth century France. And this allowed them to infer that she would be a brilliant girl in her present life, with more or less aristocratic and artistic inclinations, probably apt to becoming a writer. She would also be very sensitive to cultural and spiritual matters. And that is exactly what is happening to her now. The parents of children with such tendencies of remembering past lives, should not worry about identifying the personalities their children had in previous lives. It is better to leave things as they are in most cases. As we have seen, it is not without a reason that we forget our memories from former incarnations. It's really much better for us. But if we are led to situations or people with which we were acquainted or lived with, in former existences, whether they are famous or anonymous, we should not become too impressed with the situation. The important thing is to give shelter and love to the people who come back to nest among us, so that each and every one of us can complete the tasks we have come to perform in this present life. We should have this in order to continue the evolutionary program that has been planned out for us. Everything is related to a mysterious and subtle texture that we shall only understand later, in the same way that it is impossible to understand the whole tapestry if you look at only one of its stitches.

Readers should not allow themselves to be too impressed by revelations or confirmations. Parents should try to act naturally and to show moderate interest but not excessive curiosity as this could inhibit the child or awaken emotions and tendencies that are better left alone, in the level Myers calls subliminal. Parents should leave these things at the threshold of consciousness without disturbing such consciousness as it will be much needed in this life's work.

Whether we are conscious or not of the collection of experiences that are part of our integral memory, everything interacts and contributes in such a way that the result is the one that best suits our evolutionary process.

If a child begins to talk about previous existences; about the parents and siblings she had, how she lived and dressed, don't worry! Don't punish or discourage her, don't press her to say more than she knows or wants to. Let her talk; listen to her with attention and respect. Don't make fun of her, don't punish or get angry at her. Listen to the child, say something, and show that you think what she is saying is important. Even when you think that her words are the result of a vivid imagination the core of the story is usually true. Children are naturally endowed with a sincere purity, especially when they assume a serious, almost solemn demeanor. Always remember that you are before a spirit with a reasonable level of maturity, who knows very well what it's talking about, and who is stuck in a body which doesn't allow it to express itself fully. A child does not have a reasonable vocabulary to express itself; neither does its brain function as well as that of an adult's.

Therefore, let the child speak freely. Listen affectionately to what she has to say, and when possible help the child clarify any obscure points in her stories. It is possible that she will give clues to understanding some hidden aspects of her personality, which will enable you to help her preparing herself to follow the path she will choose for her life.

There is another aspect that should be emphasized. Children presenting these phenomena tend to be extremely sensitive, because, in spite of the limitations of their still immature bodies, they are capable of expressing much of what goes on in the depth of their souls. This means that they can at the same time have potential psychic abilities for which parents should be ready and well-informed about.

And this is what we will talk about in the next chapter.

Chapter 16.
BEING A MEDIUM IS NOT A TRAGEDY

Allan Kardec, who is precise and concise, defined a medium "as the person who acts as a channel in the communication between spirits and people in this life."

Let´s mimic Kardec's style, as we don't have time to deal with all the aspects of the subject that is mentioned here just as a necessary introduction to this chapter. The reader can choose from an array of books that deal with the subject which will provide extensive information on the psychic phenomena, the first being *The Book of Mediums* by Allan Kardec. It would be nice if the reader read my book *The Diversity of Charismas,* where the subject is explored in depth.

It is quite possible that the reader has a child in his family who is potentially endowed with the necessary sensibility "to become a link between spirits and people alive" as Kardec said.

To be a medium is to have a special kind of sensibility or perception that allows access to some type of communication between us, living people, and the invisible beings from the spiritual world. The reader should bear in mind that the children mentioned in the above cases were spirits and could not be seen, heard or perceived by ordinary people before they were born as they were still "on the other side of life". They could only be seen by those who are psychic. For one, I, myself, have never seen a spirit, and as I often say, if it depended on my actually seeing or hearing anything I wouldn't accept any of this. Fortunately this is not factual, because natural phenomena have nothing to do with our beliefs or skepticism; they simply are what they are.

So, if by chance a child in your family or in a friend's family begins to show psychic tendencies, don't panic! Don't try to repress these tendencies because it would only complicate matters unnecessarily. As we have said before, being a medium is having a special kind of sensibility or perception which enables some people to detect aspects of life that are normally beyond our regular five senses. A healthy, calm and well-balanced person, who has been reasonably instructed on such phenomena, will be prepared to deal with them in an adequate and useful way.

So, please, do not react with fear, worry or show any kind of hostility if you meet a child with the potential of becoming a medium. Let it come naturally. Do not force it to mature before its time and do not try to make the child stop. Just observe the child's behavior, being careful not to frighten it. It is by no means a disgrace to have children endowed with psychic abilities. Actually, it is a potential blessing if the child grows up in a well-balanced environment and brought up by people with common sense. After all, spirits are people just like us, and we were all spirits before. So, why shouldn't we search for ways to maintain a useful exchange with the spirits on the other side by using mediums as channels that nature created for this purpose?

With this in mind, if a child says he is seeing things or people you cannot see, or hearing voices or sounds you can't hear, don't worry and jump to the quick and false conclusion that he is going crazy. Keep calm, observe the child, think about what's going on and ask someone who is familiar with these phenomena to help you. Avoid any unwise impulsive behaviors, such as reprimanding the child, prohibiting it do what it has to do. Do not punish or threaten the child by shouting at it or intimidating it.

Most mediums in activity started showing their psychic abilities in their childhood as sporadic and fragmented displays of their sensitivity. There are reports from some reliable mediums to attest to this fact. The reader may easily have access to many well-documented reports about the initial stages of psychic phenomena in children, some of which were surrounded by adults who were clueless as to what they should do in a case like this. These people lacked the understanding and acceptance to the phenomena that the gifted children were presenting. It is possible that there are some sad stories that must have caused lifelong conflicts.

Even when the family ignores the origin or the nature of such apparently strange phenomena, it should be prepared to deal with them by being understanding and using common sense, avoiding unnecessary exaggerations.

A child is very rarely a compulsive liar. If it claims it's seeing a certain person or hearing words that make sense, give it your

CHAPTER 16.

attention. This is necessary because it will need your attention even if it really is lying.

Let us now examine the case of Divaldo Franco.

He was about four years old - this was one of his oldest memories - when a lady approached him, and asked him to deliver a message to his mother, saying:

"Tell Anna that I am Maria Senhorinha"

The boy had no idea of what a spirit was, and that spirits can be seen by certain people and talk to them. To him this was some lady asking him to give his mother Anna a message.

Divaldo did what "the lady" had asked him to do. Surprisingly, Maria Senhorinha was Anna Franco's mother, and thus Divaldo´s grandmother. Neither the boy nor his mother had ever met Maria Senhorinha "alive", because she had died giving birth to Anna, who had been raised by her elder sister Edwiges.

Anna Franco tried to discourage the boy from telling these stories, telling him that Maria Senhorinha had been his grandmother and had long been dead, and therefore could not be around (to her understanding) sending her messages. Dead people, she believed, do not talk to the living.

However, Anna Franco was impressed with the conviction the boy showed about the vision he had had, and also because he had been manifesting similar phenomena with increasing frequency. She then decided to do something different. Thinking that there was a chance this was true she took him by the hand and went to visit her sick bedridden sister.

Divaldo was asked to tell his aunt the whole story of the vision which he did very well, being limited only by his childish vocabulary. He repeated the message he had been asked to deliver in exact terms.

He described "the lady" he had met. She was a skinny woman and had green eyes. She was wearing a white dress with frills, long sleeves and a very high collar. Her hair was tied up in an old fashioned knot at the back of her head.

Aunt Edwiges did not have to talk, because tears rolled down her face. A short sentence was enough: "Anna, it's our mother!" she exclaimed.

This was the first proof that Divaldo had the makings of a medium. Anna Franco, despite not having been prepared for such an unexpected revelation, had been born with common sense and intelligence, although she was poor and uneducated. She did not allow this unusual situation to impress her much; she felt no fear, but the rest of the family, especially Divaldo's older brothers, didn't agree. To them, their little brother was kind of crazy.

Sometime later Divaldo began to have a regular playmate. The boy was approximately his size and seemed to be exactly his age. They would play, go out and talk all the time. The only problem - if that can be called a problem - was that no one, except Divaldo, could see or hear his friend, and this did not surprise or cause him any problems. They would play together pulling a string with old clothes irons attached to them pretending they were cars. The only difference Divaldo noticed was that his "car" left a track, and his friend's did not. When asked about that," the boy" gave Divaldo an explanation that seemed acceptable at the time, and the matter was definitively closed.

When talking to others Divaldo would always mention his invisible friend. To him he was a child like any other.

It is not always that these phenomena shown by some children develop in a planned way to this or that type of psychic ability. Just like the ability to remember past lives, they can disappear when the child is around ten years old. Also not everyone who is endowed with a psychic ability is destined to carry out specific missions in this area, that is, they are not *necessarily* programmed to *promote* the communication between spirits and incarnated people on a regular basis. But if they decide to devote themselves to such a responsibility, they will need the understanding and support of the people around them in order to fulfill their duties which were obviously decided in the invisible world where they had lived between lives on this earth . If parents and other relatives and friends fail to provide a sound guidance to a child showing psychic abilities, they should at least try to be understanding and to show some solidarity towards the young person that starts manifesting phenomena that are indeed unusual, but that are by no means unnatural or a sign of a mental or emotional disorder. Being a medium is by no means a tragedy. On the contrary, it is a blessing given to special people which gives them the capacity to perform the very noble function of being a link that unites the two sides of life,

CHAPTER 16.

thus allowing incarnated and pure spirits to communicate through the fictitious barrier of death.

What can be truly tragic is the stubborn resistance that many people have to serve their fellow human beings by using the noble faculties they were endowed with and who consequently spend their whole lives suffering from emotional and psychic maladjustments that result from their refusal to accept things as they really are.

Please consider any sign your child gives that it has the talent to become a medium in the same way you would react if he had revealed an inclination to any other type of talent. If your son or daughter showed a special talent for music, literature, science or sports you would normally do everything in your power to help him or her to follow a path leading to the fulfillment of their dreams and aspirations. Why not behave in the same way when the specific signs point to psychic abilities in a child?

It is also important to mention that a medium can do this work without it interfering in any other normal, healthy and honest activity a person has. Being a medium is not a profession, and does not require exclusive full time dedication. To my knowledge the best mediums were always able to juggle for many years, their role in society and their professional activities, with regular and disciplined work in well-balanced and oriented groups dedicated to spiritual exchanges.

A very close friend of mine who was very intelligent and wise was able to successfully carry out his career as a top executive in a large bank, and to practice his gift as a medium.

And so did many mediums like Chico Xavier, Waldo Vieira, Divaldo Franco, Yvonne Pereira and Zilda Gama, to mention a few . Chico retired after many years of working as a civil servant in the state of Minas Gerais. Waldo Vieira was a dentist and later a physician, at the same time as he "worked" as a medium. Divaldo worked until he retired as a social security employee. Zilda Gama was a school teacher and as far as I know so was Yvonne Pereira. None of them were professional mediums and their work did not interfere with their lives or with any of their other interests.

Once the potential to become a medium manifests itself in a child, this child and her immediate family become responsible for this. It becomes a necessity to accept, understand, and realize what is going on and to be able to help the child follow this new path over time and in the right time. The child, however, should not be reprimanded or laughed at.

In the next chapter I am going to write about a child who showed psychic tendencies at an early age. The wise and sensible attitudes of the child's mother, even though she was not familiar with spiritual matters, will be very useful to our studies, because she was intelligent enough to ask for the help of a very well-informed friend whom she trusted.

Chapter 17.
DOM BIAL AND HIS FRIEND BLATFORT

He was born healthy and physically perfect, weighing 4.2 kg; a boy that seemed happy and calm. But soon, he started being quite agitated in his sleep, as if he were having nightmares. When he was three months old he mumbled in his sleep and even crawled, a thing he couldn't do when he was awake.

It was then, while still a small boy who was unable to speak properly, that he began reacting with horror to any kind of rage or violence. Even a simple heated discussion would make him panic, become pale and start crying. Another aspect of this traumatic situation was the extreme fear he showed at any noise that might sound as gunshots. Not only did he react by showing his fear but also by becoming pale, stiff and speechless. Once, when he was a little older, he was terrified when he heard fireworks in his neighborhood and after his father assured him everything was well he said:

"Baby was sitting when brother came in and bang, bang, bang!"

As he said these dramatic words he held up his little fingers as if to mimic a gun. One can well imagine how the father felt hearing such words from an eighteen- month-old baby.

His fears and reactions went on for many years whenever he saw a gun, even toy guns which unaware parents give their kids.

"Mummy" the boy asked "policeman has a gun? Gun kill! Policeman kill baby?"

He needed to be reassured that the policeman wasn't there to kill "baby".

When the boy was about six, he ran into the house in fear and jumped into his mother's lap. Moments later, a little eight-year-old girl came in with a plastic toy gun in her hand. They had been playing cops and robbers and she was pointing the gun at him.

The mother didn't know how to handle the boy's screaming and became anxious and worried. She then mentioned her concerns to a friend who explained that the causes for this could only be accounted for as being the result of bad events happening in one of the boy's previous lives. She said that it was likely this boy had been shot and killed by a gun and this memory followed him to his present life. She insisted that the parents shouldn't reprimand the boy and should instead talk to him in an adult way. The woman volunteered to do this in the mother's presence.

"Flávio", she began. "People live many lives. A person is born, grows up, grows old, dies and is reborn. You were killed with a gun or some kind of fire arm but that was long ago in another life. You were reborn and now you have a new life. In this life nobody is going to kill you again with a weapon. You don't have to be afraid."

"Then I have already died, Didi?" said the boy.

"Yes dear, you did!" she answered.

"Someone killed me and I was born again?" asked the boy. "And nobody is going to kill me again?"

"Of course not!" replied the friend. "Now you have your daddy, your mummy and I and we won't let anybody kill you."

"Was I born again, from mummy's belly?" He asked.

"Yes" she replied.

The child understood what was explained to him in a natural way and was able to figure some things out on his own.

In fact, the idea of being reborn seemed to interest the boy very much as he started asking about the subject over and over. He was much calmer and even admitted touching a toy gun, although he never asked to have one himself.

On his first birthday, Flávio revealed another trauma connected to his former life memories. He behaved normally until a brief moment before everyone sang "Happy Birthday." He became very pale and nervous and started shouting and crying and sobbing nonstop. The family friend, Didi, whom everyone and even the child considered to be his second mother picked up André in her arms and took him to her nextdoor apartment. The boy took a long time to calm down, was visibly depressed and went into a heartfelt and continuous cry, the

CHAPTER 17.

only way he could express his deep emotions.

That incident was then dismissed as a natural fear caused by all the noise and agitation of a party, his first one, and was soon forgotten.

However, on his second birthday party-this time in his own home–(the first party had been at his grandmother's), it happened again much to everyone's distress. His mother and grandmother who did not know how to handle the situation, started crying too. Once again Didi picked up André, took him to her house and tried to calm him down for a long time. Didi decided to have a serious conversation with his mother. She concluded that undoubtedly there must have been a highly traumatic event in the boy's memory, tied to that type of party, and especially to the moment when all the guests seemed to assume a more solemn attitude. It was even possible that his death by murder, that he used to mention in his child language, had happened during a similar birthday or wedding celebration in a previous life. Whatever it was, from then on, birthday parties had everything there is to it except for candles, singing and solemn moments.

But André's behavior didn't only happen at his own parties. Even at others' parties André suffered because of his personal drama. When people started preparing to sing "Happy Birthday" he would run away and hide in a corner where he would be found feeling sad and sometimes in tears.

When André turned four, his mother decided to put an end to the boy's misery. Much against his will, the boy obeyed his mother and went with her to a party. He followed her from a distance, showing that he didn't want to go to his friend's party, when his mother turned back to wait for him and saw that tears were rolling down his cheeks.

"What's going on son?" "Are you crying?" asked the mother.

"Yes mummy. You know I don't like parties, but you are making me go... so I am going." the boy said.

That was enough to make the mother understand how bad that boy felt. She bent down, dried his tears and said:

"No, dear son, you don't *have* to go, if you really don't want to. Let's go home, and from now on I am not going to make you go to any parties you don't want to go to." she said, much to his relief.

When Flávio turned eight he managed to overcome his fears and accepted to have a small party with the happy birthday song and the works although he preferred informal gatherings with his family and a few friends.

The little boy had a strong personality. He was firm, self confident and even bossy. He didn't like being reprimanded and had little tolerance when people didn't live up to their promises even if they were simple in nature. He expected the same from himself towards others. He was very polite and righteous and had aristocratic manners. When he was just eighteen months old, he already ate by himself, and when he turned two, he used to sit at the table like an adult using the silverware and napkins correctly. It is true that his mother had a lot to do with all this, because she always treated her children with respect and attention although she knew how to use her authority when it was called for. And it is important to say that the children adapted perfectly to their mother's behavior.

Fragments from former lives seemed to surface in Flávio´s mind surely as a result of day to day situations. For instance, since he was two years old he would often repeat a word (or was it more than one?) that sounded like *"Dombial"*. When asked what it meant, he answered calmly:

"It's baby, baby is "Dombial"!" he replied.

Could it have been a Spanish nobleman known as "Don Bial" or "Vial"? But what matters is that Flávio was sure that he had been that person. His mother remembers that one day he stopped playing and sat by the radio that was playing classical music, an opera. Since he was a fan of pop music, she asked:

"What's going on, sweetie? You don't like this kind of music..."

"Yes" the boy answered. Now baby doesn't like it but when baby was "Dombial" he liked it very much!"

On a different day he seemed to be deep in meditation, and when asked what he was thinking about, he explained he was thinking about *his* hometown that was very far away; a very beautiful place that was occasionally covered in white. He then made a wide gesture with his arms, as if to describe a vast area covered by a blanket of snow.

Flávio was often disturbed by hostile spiritual beings. As we have seen before they would interfere with his sleep causing him to have

CHAPTER 17.

nightmares, walk in his sleep and even crawl, as a baby. Even his mother who had no experience in spiritual matters, seemed to detect the presence of invisible beings around his cradle trying to disturb him. Her spiritist friend advised her to have "mental conversations" with these people trying to calm them and asking them to leave her son alone as he was only a helpless little baby.

Whether the spirits decided to comply with the mother's request, or because they were sent away, the fact is that things calmed down. It is a fact though, that Flávio could see these spirits, using his psychic abilities, as it was proved in many other opportunities.

Even when he was a baby, unable to speak, Flávio seemed to "see" things that scared him, with his little finger pointing in a direction where his parents could see nothing.

But there were also invisible friends that seemed to protect him and keep him company. At a very early age, between one and half and three years old, he used to play with "someone" who would sit in a certain armchair in the living room. The mother got very nervous and tried to dissuade him without success by changing the furniture around. Flávio continued to act as if there was someone there with whom he could talk in some misterious way. One day the mother had just given him his bottle and was trying to put him to sleep, when he turned to the armchair and smiled. She changed positions and continued to try to lull him to sleep, quite anxious to make him forget whatever he was seeing in the armchair when she suddenly remembered she had left a pot on the stove and left briefly to go to the kitchen. When she returned she stopped short at the room's entrance.

The little boy was standing up in front of the armchair with his little hands resting on an invisible lap, while he happily looked towards the upper part of the armchair, as if looking at "someone" who was sitting there.

This time the mother couldn't stand it and started crying.

On the next day, still shocked by what had happened, she went to see her neighbor, friend and confident. Again she started crying, releasing all the stress she had tried to hold for a long time and told her friend all about the strange things that had been going on with Flávio. To her understanding there was only one explanation to what was happening: her dear baby was a little "nutty" She had come looking for help, as something had to be done, and soon, because things couldn't go on like this.

"It was terrible", she said," to see my son with his hands on an invisible lap, smiling at a person who wasn't there."

Didi tried to calm her by saying that although this person was invisible to her she did exist. She promised to help her, although she didn't know what to do at the moment. Later, she decided to have a mental conversation with the invisible person, whom she believed intuitively to be the boy's great-grandmother. That is approximately what she told the spirit:

"Listen, I know that you're here to help and protect little Flávio. I know you don't mean him any harm but his mother doesn't know that. She doesn't understand these things and all this is scaring her. So, please talk to her, whenever you can and explain what's going on. She has come to me for help but only you can really help her. Please talk to her and calm her down. I will be very grateful to you for this.

This short conversation" happened at night just before bedtime. On the following day, the boy's mother went back to see her friend. She was extremely happy, her eyes shining and she immediately asked:

"You did *something*, didn't you?"

And she told her the news. She had gone to bed the night before, and was almost asleep when suddenly she saw herself at her mother's home. Her grandmother was sitting on an armchair and Flávio was sitting in her lap.

"Oh, grandma, is that you?" she asked.

Now I would like the reader to please compare what the grandmother answered, to what Didi had mentally asked her:

"Yes it's me, my dear" she began. "I brought you here to assure you that I am here to help and protect our little Flávio. But it's not fair that you're so upset. If you're still upset I will have to leave.

Saying that, she put the boy down and he ran to the backyard while the two of them walked to the porch.

"You see?" asked the grandmother. "He will be there playing, and I will take care of him for you. You can relax and trust me, my dear."

CHAPTER 17.

A moment later the boy's mother woke up. It was only then, after this report, that Didi told her friend what she had asked the spirit. And the boy's mother started crying, but this time they were tears of joy. It was only her grandmother helping her take care of her son, and not a hallucination the boy had had.

There was another mysterious character that seemed to make Flávio remember bits and pieces of another past life. It was a boy who also couldn't be seen by the rest of the family as in the above case of Divaldo Franco. His name was Blatfort and in Flavio's opinion he was the only one who could pronounce this name correctly.

As it seems, the spirit showed himself to Flavio as a boy his own age. They played and talked all the time, and even argued at times. We don't know if the quarrels were between them or with another boy who played with them. Sometimes they would tease Flávio by hiding one of his toys, or by not allowing him to play with them. And he would immediately complain to his mother:

"Mummy, the boy won't give me my car!" he cried.

At that point the mother was more familiar with the situation and reacted more calmly to these phenomena thanks to her friend Didi who often talked to her. Instead of worrying or punishing her son, she just acted as if what was happening was something very natural (and it really was)

"Flávio" she said. "Let the boy play with your toy for a little while. He will give it back to you later."

Blatfort could be indiscrete at times. Once he told Flávio what his mother was cooking for him as a surprise but he was usually mature and calm. On Flávio's first day of school when he was feeling scared of the unknown something amazing happened. Flávio had been very reluctant to go to school but he finally gave in. But, when he left school he seemed perfectly calm. He told his mother:

"Do you know who was there, Mom?" "Blatfort"! "He told me not to be afraid and that going to school would be good for me."

His mother became a bit anxious. What if the teacher finds out about this Blatfort person? But it seems that the invisible friend only appeared in school on that first day, obviously just to encourage Flávio, who later complained that Blatfort was not going to school with him...

When the boy was nine years old something serious happened. Flávio came to his mother crying and feeling very anxious which in turn made her nervous. She asked her son what had happened, and he said in despair:

"I saw Blatfort!" he shouted.

"So, why are you crying, son?" she asked him.

"I saw him, mother, and he is no longer a child. Now he is a grown man, and he said he will not appear to me anymore. I won't see him again!" he cried.

Of course the mother didn't know how to deal with this strange situation. It seems that the spirit felt that it had completed its mission which was to help his incarnated friend, and that it was time to let him make his own decisions and follow his own path. He had appeared to him in his true form, that of an adult and mature spirit (if such words can be used to define a spirit) in order to say goodbye. Other possibilities were that he was about to be reincarnated into a new life on earth, or that he would continue looking after Flávio, but no longer as the constant companion who had always been around.

The psychic abilities Flavio possessed could easily be witnessed by his constant communication with spiritual beings. Not only could he see these beings but he could also talk and play with them. He used to know about things and facts that had never been revealed to him, and even those that had been deliberately kept from him.

Once, a drunken beggar who lived near his family's summer home, was run over by a car and died. Flávio used to like this man and when he disappeared the family said he had died from an illness to avoid shocking him. Flávio first seemed to accept the white lie but, a few days later; he started demanding the truth from his parents. It wasn't true that the man had been sick.

"He did not die from illness" he firmly declared. "He told me. He was going to cross the street and was run over by a car. He died but he is still there in his house. And every day he goes to the bar, as he used to do."

Mediums can usually have premonitions. Once Flávio insisted that the family shouldn't get on a certain bus that would cross a 13 km. bridge that links Rio de Janeiro to Niterói. He said they should wait for the next one, because the first bus would break down

CHAPTER 17.

halfway across the bridge. And this is exactly what happened.

Another one of Flávio's prophecies was when the family went out in a van, and he said that it would get stuck due to a big rain puddle. "But how can that be?" asked the others "On such a beautiful day?" But the boy was right: on the way back, his uncle, who was driving the van, decided to take a shortcut and fell into a big mud puddle, and they were stuck there for a long time.

A similar fact happened when little Flávio managed to convince his father to postpone a long bus trip across state lines. The father had already bought the tickets, but the boy insisted that if he took that bus he wouldn't come back alive. The bus was indeed involved in a serious accident and many passengers had died, among which a relative of a famous folk singer.

Sometime later Flávio had a premonition that his uncle would win a car in a raffle, and that it would be a black car. (he seemed to be able to see it). The uncle, who had bought a raffle ticket and had forgotten all about it, won the prize: a black car.

Flávio announced the birth of a cousin, and added that it would be a girl even before her mother knew she was pregnant.

As I am writing these notes, Flávio is almost thirteen. He is perfectly normal; a healthy, strong and very bright boy. He taught himself to read using learning toys and games. At school he is a fast learner, and breezes through his classes. (It is not without a reason that Socrates said that learning is no different from remembering.) His dear Didi, an experienced teacher, is under the impression that the present educational system doesn't allow him to develop to his fullest potential.

Modern research shows that a super gifted child ends up by suffering from the deficient education offered .This child will not find at school the necessary stimulus and challenge so important for its cultural development, nor the necessary freedom to make a better choice of subjects as far as its curriculum is concerned. .

Truly, intelligence is not a special gift, nor something that you can genetically inherit, but the proof that the spirit has lived longer, has more experience, is more mature and has already dealt with several different problems, having therefore acquired more wisdom in its many lives.

One day we will learn how to deal with these special people, many of which are stuck and lost in anonymity, because they lacked the necessary motivation at the right moment. But, in spite of this, there are many of them who succeed in overcoming all obstacles and even go on opening new paths for those following behind.

It makes sense to hope that Flávio will be one of these special people.

The important lesson learned here comes from the excellent relationship among the people around Flávio: his parents, siblings and Didi, their friend. Such problems and difficulties could have been the source of panic or of conflicts that could be regretted. Inversely, they were handled in a wise and calm way once the normal perplexity and emotional impact of the beginning were overcome.

It's worth mentioning that a combination of lucky circumstances led to rational solutions for the crises at hand. The mother, who was not trained to deal with normal but strange and stressful situations that can occur in the human psyche, was lucky to find someone whom she trusted entirely, who was capable of guiding her in the right way. However, the results and consequences of such facts might not have had a positive outcome had the person chosen to guide them been a phony "expert" offering readymade solutions for this kind of situation.

Therefore, let us now renew the recommendations that we have made several times in this book: do not panic if your child starts remembering former incarnations, or displaying a psychic behavior. Keep calm, give the child your attention, process everything in a calm way, ask questions in a natural way. Show your child that you love and understand him and assure him that you will be there to protect him when he is afraid. Never make threats or punish the child for "making things up". After that, try looking for people who are familiar with these situations. But before you start doing what the person tells you to, you should really trust this person as well as his (or hers) knowledge and methods.

This is the critical point in the whole process, because there are many people who claim to have a vast knowledge of spiritual matters, but who are nothing more than curious, unprepared people who teach wrong things about spiritism and have no more than just a shallow idea of such matters.

CHAPTER 17.

Mediumship is a psychic gift and not a mental illness or emotional unbalance. It is rather a special sensibility, a noble and special skill that once well directed and trained, will serve as a wonderful channel of communication between incarnate beings and the beings that, at the moment, are living in a world invisible to us.

The best thing to do: calm down! Also another very important thing, learn to pray, if you still don't know how.

Chapter 18.
THE MUCH DISCUSSED INFLUENCE OF THE ENVIRONMENT

All of us wish to have children that are handsome, healthy and intelligent. Usually this is what happens, but not always. An anxious father once came to me for advice. He was scared because his young son displayed, from an early age, signs of a fantastic intellectual endowment. Not only was the child extremely intelligent but also exceptionally mature. It was not difficult to understand why that sensible father was worried, as he was aware of the duty he and his wife faced of educating the little genius who had come to their family. "How should one raise a child like this one?" he asked. "How should we educate and guide him? How can I help my son develop his full potential?"

As I see it, his concern is legitimate because intelligence alone is neutral, that is to say, it can either be used for good or for evil purposes. It may be an instrument of evil minds or, on the other hand, it may be an element devoted to good causes that will always leave fraternal love and happiness in its path.

I don't know why, but my intuition about that boy was the best possible. I suggested that the anxious father and his wife should give their son all the material and moral support he needed and devote their utmost love to him. As to the path the boy would follow in life, they needn't worry, because he was certainly aware of the mission he had come to accomplish here among us. I explained to him the mechanism of rebirth as best I could, trying to make him understand that a child is not a novice in this life, but someone resuming the continuous road toward perfection. Children come from past eras and are always evolving.

I could not hope that the father would accept everything I had told him, because he was an extremely Catholic man who believed in the Catholic notions which I felt I should respect.

CHAPTER 18.

I was, however, under the impression that he had left feeling more at peace. I can remember details of that day. It was late in the afternoon, and it was beginning to get dark. We had recently moved to a new apartment that was being reformed, and our house was quite a mess.

Today, as I am writing this book, 15 years have passed and the boy is now a young man over twenty. All the positive expectations I had about him have been confirmed, and the modest and involuntary "prophecies" came true. He really *knew* (and knows) how to find paths leading to the fulfillment of his destiny and is trying them out successfully. He is really endowed with a superior intelligence and is an excellent student. He is very serious and isn't afraid to tackle difficult matters which would apparently scare people older than him away. Being a young polyglot, his readings cover a wide variety of topics, but he knows how to be selective, and as such he focuses on what is really important.

Although he is part of a bigger picture he manages to keep well balanced emotions and doesn't allow himself to become an insensitive intellectual, who wants nothing but more and more knowledge. He is a loving son who is extremely devoted to his parents, and has an excellent relationship with them.

All in all he is a very mature and experienced spirit and we can clearly perceive that he has had a succession of long and successful lives. Wherever or whenever he is reborn, he will find his way, overcoming all larger or smaller difficulties no matter which conditions he will have to face.

And this leads us to the discussion of a theme that has been the source of innumerable discussions, both technical and speculative: are human beings in general and children particularly, mere *results of their environment*? Or in other words, are we molded by the environment, or do we impose ourselves to it, developing virtues or vices, in spite of what is happening around us in this or that sense ?

The experience and observation of factors that haven't yet been considered by official science - which does not consider important elements of the problem, such as the spiritual reality - induce us to give careful answers which may be confirmed or rejected. This is a basic requirement for almost every human problem.

Only seldom can human problems be tackled and solved by

means of readymade mathematical formulas which cover all situations of the same nature. In only a few very specific cases can human beings be quantified and classified, this belonging rather to the realm of statistics. It's possible to find out exactly how many men, women and children live in each community, their age groups, their schooling, or their financial status. We can find out what religion they follow, what their line of work is, what kind of housing they possess. But how can we possibly determine their degree of happiness, their feelings, or to what extent brotherly love leads them to this or that action?

The old debate about the influence of the environment on people could be placed in less radical terms. It would not be wise to deny that the environment influences people, because it's impossible to deny the human imitation impulse which is present especially in children. Children usually try hard unconsciously or consciously to imitate one or both parents, in one or more traits of their personalities. They can get used to speaking loudly, to preferring certain types of food, to accumulating material things instead of searching for intellectual growth. All these things are a result of the imitation stimulus, or the simple lack of environmental motivation.

On the other hand, however, it isn't hard to find children who are excellent students and strive to learn more and more despite the lack of motivation they have gotten from their environments. In the same way we can find young people brought up among intellectuals who choose a totally different line of activity from the one they grew up with.

We can therefore conclude that specific gifts or tendencies may be either stimulated or evoked as well as smothered by the influence of the environment but that there are children who react to this environment in a stronger or weaker way.

It is not, therefore, the environment we live in that makes in a final, unquestionable and inevitable way a person to be this or that way. It can, however, contribute by adding some touches of color to the person's behavior.

Let us repeat: a child is a spirit who, not long ago, was a part of the invisible world which lies between carnal lives and was recently reborn into a new incarnate existence. Between one life and the next we go through a period of personal appraisal where past actions are evaluated and concepts are restructured and our life program is planned. All in all, what have we done up to now, what did we do wrong or right, what do we need to do to develop this or that evolutionary line? How to fix past mistakes? What should be done to recover lost affections that resulted from our insanity? How can we make amends with those we have made our enemies? What tasks will we have to perform in the next incarnation or the ones after that? Which negative traits should we eliminate and which ones should we develop? Where, when and next to who will we be reborn next time? What will our goal be concerning our work and personal plans?

After considering all of the above points and many other complex ones and once we have found a priority scale we finally elaborate a program for action with the help of devoted and competent advisors. This life program takes many variables into account. All and all, however, one has the chance to exercise free will which is respected by cosmic laws. These laws guide us and are quite flexible although not random and undefined. In extreme cases the law interferes with this free will by using a curbing device which stops someone from performing wrong acts in future lives. An example of this: after many unsuccessful lives where one makes the same mistakes over and over it is possible for the cosmic laws to interfere by forcing a spirit to incarnate into a handicapped body or to live a vegetative life in order to, paradoxically, protect this person from herself and her insanity. It's as if the law determined a so called "life imprisonment" because it will last while one's life lasts and might even overflow from one life to the next and beyond that.

As a child is a spirit who carries a program, a plan, a project which must be executed it is even possible that it might be sent into a hostile environment precisely because it did not perform its task due to negligence, lack of responsibility or lack of interest when it had the adequate resources to do so.

However, in order to evaluate parents' or tutors' difficult position and in order to understand all this we should show other aspects that illustrate this complex situation.

Suppose the child comes into its new life with a heavier load of deficiencies and mistakes to fix? It isn't hard to imagine that in a case like this the spirit is still somewhat rebellious, maladjusted or lacking in harmony and then will its environment play a very important part in this process. If it meets people who can help combat its negative tendencies, this child may be more successful than if otherwise those around would not help, letting it follow its own instincts or even contribute to perpetuate the negative tendencies it is programmed to lessen or even completely correct.

All this said, we can infer that the task of raising a child is a very serious matter, be it your own or someone else's. If one contributes to the aggravation of its negative tendencies instead of helping it to overcome them one will assume additional quotas of responsibility towards that child and will be making the relationship with this being worse in the short or long run in this life or in future lives. We are not psychological or emotional islands. We are particles of one and only continent of life. Whatever we do or fail to do, however strange it may seem, might change things which may only be solved in hundreds or thousands of years. As the modern mystic-physicists say (See *Tao in Physics* by Fritjof Capra) the almost unnoticeable movements made by our tiny individual atom, as we are particles of consciousness, trigger corresponding movements in the cosmos in which we are integrated. Anyway, if we act well or not, we create a disturbance or an adaptation of the universe as a whole. No other phenomenon is as fantastic and impressive to humans as that of the so-called cosmic consciousness, a state that has been described as being similar to a feeling of ecstasy, which generates in the human being the certainty of being integrated and participating in a whole. The bits and pieces we have of testimonies on this, account for the feeling of perfect global identity as if the individual were the whole universe and not only a conscious atom.

All this, however, would be the material for another book. What we want to stress here is the responsibility we have over a child's development, whether it's our own biological child or adopted. Truly, to be precise, this responsibility recedes far back as it starts at the moment where, for one or other reason our destinies have crossed somewhere far away in time, difficult for us to determine or even imagine when. Karmic problems that are still today being worked at, and may continue for centuries or millennia may have been woven in the tapestry of eternity since times that only our integral memory may reveal.

My book *The Exiled* describes the memories of a spirit that already had problems to solve when he was brought to reincarnation on earth due to persisting mistakes made in remote areas of the universe.

CHAPTER 18.

Therefore that handsome, healthy, intelligent son we have now can be a friend from faraway eras, who has honored us by granting us the joy and the responsibility of being his parents. Let's welcome this son with the happiness we deserve, and with all love that has joined us since long ago in the unbreakable ties of immortal light.

Chapter 19.
HANDICAPPED CHILDREN

Well, but what if the child assigned to us is not good looking, intelligent or healthy? After the greater or smaller impact caused by such a reality, our first attitude should be to consider that the person that came to us is a human being, a child of God, just as much as we are. The second attitude, just as important and urgent as the first, is to realize that the child, a spirit who is physically limited has been entrusted to our care for some plausible reason. Some of these limitations may have a solution, others may be permanent, irreversible. Our role will be that of accepting the situation to face the oncoming difficulties. The third point is to keep in mind that the divine law reserves final happiness to all of us and that all the pain, lack of harmony and maladjustments are temporary. There is no such thing in the universe as eternal suffering. Some human beings may suffer for longer or shorter periods of time, depending on the extent of their mistakes, and on the effort they put into fixing these mistakes that have broken the cosmic laws. These laws foresee and provide everything and the spirit must strive towards reaching final inner peace. Some religions refer to this as salvation. The name is not important. What counts is the truth contained therein. The fourth point that should be mentioned is that parents of a handicapped child are necessarily personally involved in the matter. In other words, they are responsible for that child although this responsibility is not always their fault. Human beings are not put into the world to suffer, to feel anxious or to feel rejected. They are put here to be happy. All the writings about cosmic laws agree on this point. We would get there if we understood that the divine laws don't work *against us* but that they work *in our favor*.

The divine laws are programmed to guide us towards the highest levels of spiritual perfection. This is why they contain the best methods of fixing our mistakes in our evolutionary scripts when we wander off the right path. This is the only way the "Supreme Intelligence" which is what spirits call Divinity can use to guide us to the right path whenever we stray from it by taking shortcuts.

It is a fact that the child that comes to us with physical or mental

CHAPTER 19.

limitations will cause much suffering to itself and to those who care for it. It is very hard for totally unprepared people to accept a situation as difficult as this one. In this case the limitations of a son or daughter we love are the remedy that the law has prescribed to the child and to the parents so that they can find the peace that is out there waiting for them.

If one chooses not to take the medicine prescribed by the law to cure such grievances things will only become worse.. The law is acting out of compassion, and not out of evil or revenge. It is providing us with the much desired chance of recovery, reconstruction, and purification.

It is true that one should go through many trials and tribulations when faced with such a situation. I am familiar with many examples of how hard this is and I am sure my readers are too.

I was particularly impressed with one case.

A boy was born apparently perfect, but soon he was no more than a vegetable. He never walked or talked, never left his bed, or better said beds, for he lived for more than thirty years. Lived? you may ask. Yes he lived, despite the fact that he was imprisoned in a body he couldn't control. He would only roll his eyes in deep frightened looks. In the rare moments he could sleep, he seemed to have terrible nightmares from which he would awake in panic, as if he wanted to safely return to his body which was a blessing and a shelter for him and not a place of suffering.

It was there in that zombie-like body that he found all the love he needed as well as the constant presence of his very devoted mother. One day she died, after an unexpected illness. A couple of months later he died. They were both free, the prisoner that he was, and his sweet caretaker, who had voluntarily chained her own feet to the same chains that tied her son to his handicapped body. She had never complained, was never desperate or revolted and never seemed tired. She even left before him so that she could be waiting for him on the other side when he got there.

Maybe one day we will get to know something about the dramatic story from former eras that caused so much suffering to these two spirits. But, even if I had been given the chance, I wouldn't want to know what had happened because these two people endured this ordeal with so much love and dignity that it deserves our greatest respect and admiration.

We can imagine that that mother's spirit had a debt to pay off to that prisoner. It is even possible that she was the cause of many of his moral deviations at a point in the past. Or it may even be that she spontaneously accepted this hard task as a means of helping someone she used to love and still loves to escape the bad situation he was in.

As I have said before, I know nothing of their story except what we can see here on this side of life. I am sure though, that if we happen to meet the glowing spirit of a serene woman, it might very well be she is that devoted mother.

Christ said, in the endless wisdom of all his teachings to us, that it is easy to love our friends, but hard to love our enemies. And this is exactly what we need to do. And we can extend this concept, by saying it is easy to love handsome, intelligent and healthy people, but, as Christ also said, healthy people don't need doctors; sick people do. And often the diseases of the soul affect exactly those with beautiful bodies and gifted minds. The fact is that beauty and intelligence, as well as power and wealth are tests we must take to know if we are mature enough to safely know the difference between permanent life values and transient, fake values. Most of all we are tested as to whether we are willing to use our wisdom and courage to make the right choices.

About this subject please let me tell you about another case I have already briefly talked about somewhere before.

A boy was born to a well-to-do, intelligent, cultivated and handsome young couple. He was also a handsome good looking child, but had no control over his body. Relatives that contacted me about this case told me that the boy's brain had been badly damaged as a result of extended oxygen deprivation at the time of his birth. He survived this experience but his brain suffered irreparable harm. In addition, a tomography revealed that his brain was too small and would allow him only the minimum to stay alive.

There is an important detail in this case. The boy's grandfather, an excellent doctor, was very sad because he couldn't do anything to save his grandson.

This type of situation brings about many distressing questions. Why? Why did this happen to my son? Or my grandson? Why couldn't I avoid this situation? How could this terrible accident been

CHAPTER 19.

avoided? Whose fault is it?

There might even be answers to some of these questions but they wouldn't help fixing the situation.

As the family wished to have a better understanding of their situation they came to us and asked us to speak to our spiritual friends. They agreed to clarify some points and bring us words of comfort and guidance.

According to them, the father, mother and son had been part of a love triangle in a past life. The young woman and one of the young men had already set the date for the wedding when she fell in love with the other one who is now the handicapped child's father. In a moment of rage the young man who was rejected by the girl jumped off a cliff and seriously damaged his physical brain. The grandfather in this life who was his father in the previous life, did everything to save him then but wasn't able to do so and suffered deeply as he truly loved his son and had high hopes for him. As for the girl she finally married the young man of her choice.

As part of the arrangements of the divine laws the three of them were joined together in this life. They planned to get married again and receive the young man who had been the man's rival and the girl's rejected fiancé. The law gave the parents the opportunity to bring that boy who had died as a result of their rivalry back to life. The abandoned groom made the serious mistake of trying to take his life and damaged one of the most important vital centers- the physical brain. This caused serious and inevitable consequences in his perispirit.

The evidences point to the fact that even if the birth had been incident-free the child would be severely brain damaged and condemned to a life subject to serious physical and intellectual limitations.

Anyway, raising that boy became a heavy burden to the parents. It was also very hard for the boy himself, as he was a prisoner of a handicapped body. His impulsive act in a former life when he had the chance of leading a healthy life in a healthy body led him to much suffering in this life. If we went further back we could have seen that in another even more distant life, a behavior flaw had put him in the position of being rejected by his fiancée who favored the other young man. None of this is a result of chance. We are never sent to a new life programmed to commit suicide, to kill or to murder or to practice any other crime. We are put here to better ourselves, to test our resistance and conquests especially under stressful conditions which our past mistakes created for us. In other words, committing suicide because of a frustrated love affair was totally useless.

He could have reformulated his life because for sure, that specific incident of his being rejected by her was more of a test, a possibility than a certainty.

The three of them complicated themselves in their relationships with the laws instead of finding solutions to fix their mistakes.

There is something peculiar about this case. Our spiritual friends who brought us the message of guidance had a meeting with the child's spirit as he was completely lucid in spiritual terms despite his handicapped body. That spirit was fully aware of its involvement in the problem and was sorry for all the pain everyone had to suffer but was willing to do his part of the deal. He asked people to treat him as normally as possible without making a big deal about his limitations. He wanted to participate as much as he could of the life around him. As he was a prisoner of his body he felt very lonely. He felt isolated both from the incarnated people as well as from the spirits. He asked them to speak to him whenever they could. Although *he was unable to talk* he *was able to understand what they told him.*

For some time I lost track of that family whose ordeal had deeply touched me. One day I heard that the boy had died. I pray for him and hope he is well now, back in the spiritual world preparing himself to return, who knows where or when or under what circumstances to follow in the direction of perfection which is what awaits all of us. Peace is further ahead, we can already see it. It will soon be here for those who have fought to achieve balance and a little bit further away for those who still have to understand that the divine law guides us slowly in the direction of peace. Let's go with the flow instead of foolishly fighting against the tide.

Let's not worry about climbing mountains to prove we are great, but rather with the sweet joy of the eternal love that illuminates the gardens of life, where no one is big or small, because everybody is pure and happy.

What lesson can then be learned from this chapter? We must understand however difficult it may seem in practice and easy to

CHAPTER 19.

know in theory, that our handicapped children are also children of God like we are. They are people with whom we had problems in the past and must help find fraternal love again. This shouldn't be done so that we can get rid of them forever, but so that we can both go ahead on our path to happiness. I often tell the spirits we communicate with that this is not easy but we sure believe it is possible. It is necessary and indispensable. It doesn't really matter where we pass on our path, what matters is that it takes us in the direction of our much desired peace which we deserve by rights of inheritance.

***

Additional note

Some chapters of this book, such as this one are like letters that require a P.S. Stories, like life, are endless because they can be rewritten at any time.

Sometime after the boy died, our spiritual friends asked me if I would like to talk to him. How could I possibly turn down this opportunity?

And one night, as we were finishing our regular spiritual session, the spirit of that boy talked through our medium. His first word was to acknowledge his gratitude for what we had tried to do to help him and his former family although we were not successful as it is indeed very hard to convince spiritually unprepared people that everything is well and in accordance with the definitive laws of life and that the key word here is *acceptance*.

As far as he was concerned he was now at peace, and as conscious as he could possibly be, considering the difficulties his physical body went through in his recently-finished life.

With his retrospective memory he could now go backwards in time and previous lives, and understand the distant causes of his behavior and experiences. He much regretted his disastrous suicide that he understood as being a rebellious gesture with tragic consequences. He added that he might have had some attenuating circumstances (he hesitated a while, choosing a word) if at least he would not have been a victim of the heavy doses of hate, specially directed against the young lady who as he saw it, had betrayed him, choosing the other one instead. Besides, he could now see how useless his desperate gesture had been, when he found out that another woman had been destined to him. And that this other woman he really loved tenderly, not just with a fleeting passion. Being rejected by that first girlfriend was just one more unpleasant experience he had to face because of prior commitments. Never does the law include suicides and tragedies.

Anyway, many lessons were learned from these dramatic events. He was informed that in his next life he would no longer endure the physical limitations that had made him a prisoner in a handicapped body in his recently-ended incarnation. He had been punished for his rebellious act. The most important thing for him, however, is that he was free from the hate he had felt for those who had led him to such an act even though he knew his gesture had been entirely his responsibility.

This is what he said about it all.

He asked: "If you can, tell those who were my parents that I love them."

Confirming what I had supposed, he declared that his physical deficiency had nothing to do with medical malpractice during his birth. He would have been born with a faulty brain, even if everything had gone well during the birth.

He then mentioned how difficult it was to repair his brain so that it could work normally after all the damage it had suffered as a result of the suicide. He explained that the damage done to the physical body might not be that important. What really matters is how this damage affects the perispirit.

Another point was also clarified: it is quite normal for the parents of a handicapped child to feel uneasy or even guilty for having produced an imperfect body for their child. This is what I felt when I was in touch with the family in this story. It was as if they were asking themselves how it was possible for healthy and handsome parents to bear an unhealthy child. Therefore their tendency to blame it on the birthing accident. In fact, this feeling of guilt had its roots in the rejection drama derived from the broken engagement which still stirred their unconscious memories.

It was also noticeable that the rejected man was angrier at the former lover who had exchanged him for someone else than with the man who had stolen her heart. (Was it my impression, or did I really detect the father's special love for his deficient baby?)

CHAPTER 19.

Just one more word: The medium, through which the boy's spirit talked to me, saw him and described him as a good looking and calm person. It was obvious that he was willing to resume his life from the point it had been interrupted by the tragedy.

He told me that he was thinking recently, to be reborn to a new experience on Earth precisely as the son of the woman who had been (and still is) his true love and with whom he was destined to marry in the other existence. But this was not allowed by the law as this same law is quite tolerant but very strict.

All in all, living a life with your loved ones is put on hold until everything is settled, as Christ has taught us.

When we parted, both of us feeling emotional, he thanked me again for everything I had tried to do to help his family. He seemed to know that I had not been successful in the endeavor. There are seeds which take longer than others to bloom but they will always produce some form of renewed life when they are able to break the barriers existing between what Aristotle calls *potency* and *act*. To many of us love is still potency, to others it has already bloomed and turned into act.

Chapter 20.
THE DRAMATIC WORDS OF A SPIRIT

More than once have we mentioned the plans that are elaborated in the spiritual world for every life that starts on Earth. There are many unimaginable details to consider regarding such plans: the past should be researched and future possibilities assessed, people with whom future activities must be negotiated should be found and contacted. The conditions under which the spirits who are programmed to perform a common task should be reborn must be carefully examined, that is to say, how should they be guided, which of their tendencies should be stimulated, which should be downplayed, which virtues emphasized, which mistakes to correct as well as verifying how much pressure they can take and which problems should be left for later lives. All in all there are many variables to be considered and evaluated so that a viable plan can be conceived within reasonable limits although not always ideal ones.

But often enough after everything has been carefully set up spirits come to the flesh and fail to do their part of the job and everything falls apart again!

Although these theoretical speculations are important, I prefer a practical, experimental approach which gives us concrete examples taken from people's lives. I believe that we can only learn to live by living and not by making theories about life.

As a lucky outcome of a network of circumstances we have had many precious opportunities through the years of "seeing" living examples of this uncomfortable truth: we are rarely able to follow through on our tasks in the flesh which were planned for us between lives, with the right amount of precision and commitment.

Once, however, a spiritual friend who had just awakened from a long nightmare of secular mistakes gave us a rich account about his experiences and mature observations which were unexpected, moving and extremely honest.

CHAPTER 20.

As I have said, he had been making serious mistakes along many lives which had been sacrificed as a result of his bad behavior. Unfortunately he's not alone in doing this as it has practically been the rule for almost all of us, up to the moment when a personal earthquake shakes the foundations of our being and we are no longer the same.

What follows is a commented summary of what he told us that night.

"Sometimes", he said, "the commitments made to the law are so serious that the spirits think that they can't fix the tragedies they are in. Too many mistakes were made in past lives. It's true that there is always someone willing to help but this person also makes mistakes. We can illustrate this by using the example of the companion who chooses to return to a life of shared difficulties. She promises to be faithful which was her greatest weakness in the past. The plan is made to allow this person to return to a carnal life and follow through with this plan. However, when she returns she betrays her man again, moved by an impulse she has not yet learned to control. And he also fails as he is once more unable to be tolerant and understanding towards other person's weaknesses.

There are times in which the programs designed to overcome problems end up by causing irreparable situations which are not the result of *disagreements* but the result of *misunderstandings* which could be easily settled. All that's needed is a time to think things over in order to prepare for a calm discussion of the problem which is not, at that point, unsolvable. Instead, tempers flare and things get complicated. Difficulties that can be easily overcome become deadlocks.

What happens is that spirits who come back on Earth with the best intentions, once reincarnated submit to the negative tendencies and start making the same mistakes and arise the same passions they came to combat and dominate. The fight for power is one example of a resistant spiritual *infection* that seems to contaminate the lives of those who were sent to Earth to improve their behavior. We are reborn to learn how to control ourselves and we end up giving in to the impulse of dominating others.

Problems start happening when we are being tested because we forget, while in the flesh, about the deals we made. These deals become nothing more than vague and distant memories.

My spiritual friend said: "They told me things that I *knew* in some way were right (or wrong), but I didn't know exactly *why*."

Many complain of this forgetfulness and blame it for making the same mistakes again. But the intention of the law is that we learn the lesson of doing good by our own means, initiatives and dispositions when faced with the many choices that present themselves to us. We have to prove to ourselves that, when faced by such or such situation we might be able to decide what to do not because we have to be right or have to make amends with this or that enemy from other eras, but because we now possess the notion of good inside of us which will help us in all future situations..

What happens is that we bring to this life the stubborn molds of evil to which we were used to before. Soon we start straying from the righteous path. Old acquaintances insist on dragging us back to crime, drinking, irresponsibility. The gifts of intelligence or mediumship are used negatively as they represent forms of power we haven't yet learned how to use for serving but instead, to dominate and oppress so that we can be served and praised. Such gifts that the law gives us to promote our betterment attract many fascinated admirers who wish to have their share of the benefits this power brings to those who possess them. Besides, it is easier to meet a person who lights up old passions in us which are just dormant than a more conscious and experienced companion who is unpleasant and we reject because he is constantly reminding us of our duties and telling us to give up many things we are not yet ready to give up.

At moments like this, I like to remind everyone of how the Gospel can inspire us when we need to find the right path to follow. Unfortunately very few people read the scriptures nowadays. People would rather criticize them.

A spiritual friend assured us that fighting the scriptures is an act of despair. Not because they are not genuine as it has been said, but because they *are* genuine.

"Evil", he said, "adjourns and is indolent. The Gospel is not."

This is why it is so convenient for these spirits who are adrift to try to create an alternative world where the laws of God can be forgotten or disobeyed at least for some time. Once this rebellious and irresponsible bubble is created many count on it to live their passions and lunacy to the fullest. They know this is a utopia that can

CHAPTER 20.

only lead to more mistakes instead of fixing the ones that have already existed for many centuries in that conscience which is dormant but not dead. But who can convince them that they are just trying to run away from themselves, an impossible deed?

What is the motivation behind all of this? It is one and only: the fear of suffering. All of those who are living according to this unfeasible life philosophy know that one day they will have to settle affairs with the upset cosmic harmony but while they are here they might as well live their fantasies and madness. They are fully aware that peace becomes further and further away and hard to reach because the road to get there is full of swamps and briar patches, deserts and difficult ground. On our way back we have to take the same road.

In his catharsis my spiritual friend added: "We were brave when making mistakes but we are cowards when we have to face the consequences of such mistakes."

On the other hand, there is an aggravating circumstance in this process. We come back to a world where it is much easier and interesting to give in to old wrong doings than to bravely resist them by living a life which is austere and severe or at least decent and restrained.

Even devoted institutions that should be doing redeeming work and promoting love among neighbors are affected by this subtle evil as they too are run by imperfect human beings who are striving much more to be in leadership positions than to seek the improvement of human beings. This applies to the large religions as well as to the many sects that are starting to pop up everywhere.

This is why the clean, active practice of mediumship, which is our link with the companions who live in the other side of life, is strongly combated. It is either combated or misinterpreted. Within the practice devoted to love, to learning, to material and spiritual guidance there is a subtle inclusion of science, psychic phenomena, embroidered psychography, which lead to deviations and delays of the paths of those who are willing to postpone their encounters with Truth. Thus, spirits who are highly misadjusted, disoriented, suddenly become very respected *mentors* and spiritual *guides* who turn out having faithful followers consulting them on every move.

It is not that such spirits are unprepared or ignorant. Conversely, they are very intelligent and experienced as the result of the long experience they have had on Earth and in the spiritual world. Besides they know divine laws extremely well and use them to their benefit as much as possible. They also know the human psyche very well and know exactly which buttons to press, which feelings to stir, which attitudes to adopt in order to get support and attention from the vain and improvident. They know people's motivations, know their past histories, their commitment with this or that episode or human being. This makes it easy for them to manipulate so many people, handle influences, promote desirable meetings and make evil plans.

My spiritual friend reported: " If I mention the Gospel they listen to me with apparent attention and respect but they can't hide how bored they really are. But if I tell them they are wonderful, intelligent, devoted and that the glories of sanctity await them everyone thinks I am wonderful and they kindly give in to my lead."

This can cause a dangerous imbalance of opposing powers as most people are still on the bad side, pulling at the rope with all their strength and fears in the direction of their negative passions.

He asks sadly: "What is the purpose of being reborn in a world like this where only a small minority is really committed to improving?

***

That is the crude and cruel reality in which our children and grandchildren are born nowadays. Which life programs should they follow? What commitments must they make? What are their weaknesses? What are the traits consolidated in their personalities? What kind of experiences have they had? What corrections do they mean to make? What can we do to help them avoid making the same mistakes they were destined to correct and erase from their psychic and ethical molds?

Chapter 21.
THE GIRL CRYING ON THE SIDEWALK

On a sunny Sunday morning we went out on our usual walk along the quiet streets of our neighborhood. About a block from our house we saw a little girl crying on the sidewalk. She was no older than three or four. She was pretty and well dressed as if she had just been dressed for an outing. A few steps away a young man looked at her in distress. She was not making a scene, just crying a heartfelt, deep cry, showing much anguish in her eyes. Before I knew what I was doing I approached her and tried to make her feel better with some kind "grandfather" words. Why was she crying, that little being who had just started a new life? I did not mean to intrude as we are all entitled to privacy but the young man commented briefly: "She wants her mother to go with us!" I didn't ask anything else and I didn't have to. I knew what was going on.

It was likely that daddy and mommy had separated. The father had been allowed to pick up his daughter on Sundays. Did he have a new girlfriend? Did mommy remarry? I don't know. They were still mommy and daddy to the little girl crying on the sidewalk but now they were no longer together. They almost never talked and barely looked at each other. They acted like enemies. Life had just started for her and already things had radically changed in her small individual universe. Suddenly things had become confusing and difficult to understand. She was probably asking herself why her mommy couldn't join them on this outing today.

Sometimes we would well like to be able to do magic tricks like in fairy tales. I would like to magically join that mother, that father and their daughter. But this would break the other triangle: that of mommy, daddy and the other woman, or who knows, daddy, mommy and the other man. Or at that moment I would like to take that child in my arms and take her somewhere daddy and mommy would never separate. But I couldn't do that and even if I could I wouldn't because I would be interfering in the freewill of the people involved. It was a painful personal drama that hurt everyone, especially the little girl whose only wish was to have her mother's company on that sunny Sunday.

All I could do was to go on my way and watch them go on theirs. Whatever the case, I took some of that pain with me and left with a thought of tenderness towards that confused child. More than that, I really had there something to think about.

As I came from a family with long lasting marriages my evaluation on this subject might not please many people and sound outdated. Both my parents and my in-laws only separated when they died. As I write these lines I can say that my own marriage has gone past 50 years. I cannot, obviously, speak for my ancestors, but we did have problems in our relationship along the way. Who doesn't? This is why we are here: to polish rough edges, correct lack of affection, develop affections, cultivate understanding, end past bitterness, dedicate and devote ourselves to others. If we give up fighting on the first or hundredth battle we are only postponing the chance for peace to an unknown future. This is because we can't buy harmony at the local drugstore or supermarket. This is a difficult and slow process that takes a whole life or maybe lives. It requires understanding, tolerance and abnegation. The home is a meeting place. This is the cosmic moment in which the right conditions were set up for everything to work out well. And if one must part after conciliation they must leave as friends which are only saying goodbye for some time, with meetings set up in the future so that they can go on with their shared projects and to new evolutionary phases as we are all travel companions. Suddenly abandoning the task of understanding each other to go on alone is a useless thing to do even if one is able to do it. Something will be missing in the future, something we failed to do when we had all the chance.

A spiritual entity told us an interesting story regarding this subject. She had been sharing her life with a companion in the evolutionary journey. At a certain point they needed to make a serious decision. Figuratively, they stopped a few steps from a door that illustrated a new phase of progress and accomplishments since they could see lights shining ahead. They talked about the situation, as he was in doubt whether to go ahead. They ended up by separating. He stayed, she went ahead. She now regretted not having insisted on staying with him a little longer until he decided to join her. She didn't insist and now they followed different paths on their own. She told us, in tears, about how wrong her decision had been.

CHAPTER 21.

They lost touch for a long time. She walked for a while in the direction of the light but he stayed behind probably because they were no longer together in the task of planning a peaceful strategy for their life.

"It's as if", she said, "you had a valuable treasure waiting for you in the future. You get there first but the lock can only be opened with two keys and you only have yours, the other belongs to the person who stayed behind. Either you wait for this person or you go back to get him so that both of you can get to that treasure."

Family is our university. We either graduate from this university with a complete masters or PhD, ready for our personal conquests, or we leave before the right time interrupting the course of hope. From what I could see in the research I made to write my part in Deolindo Amorim's book there has never been a better social cell than that of the family. I can also guarantee that there has been much experimentation. Everything has been tried, many formulas and models have been tested but the old model resists. If things aren't working out according to the experts, it is not the model that is wrong, it is people who are wrong.

As I am not an expert in this field, I'd rather not approach it. This doesn't mean, however, that I don't have my opinion regarding this subject. It is very clear to me. I believe that the formula was thrown away before it could be replaced by a new, more advantageous one. But I doubt such an alternative formula ever existed or will exist. Besides, I believe that the failure of the system started when sex and love were separated from each other. I can see in this sex/love dichotomy a broader dichotomy: the matter/spirit dichotomy in which love is tied to the spirit and sex is merely biological and aimed at guaranteeing renewed reincarnation possibilities to all. The union of these two is responsible for continuing life in the flesh and their separation creates unpredictable problems because once sex is disconnected from the spiritual component it becomes passion and instead of being the flame that brings light and warmth it will be a flame that will extinguish soon among the shadows.

While our passions come and go, blind us and are extinguished, those who chose to live with us in this dimension suffer.

Conflicts existing between parents have strong repercussions on children and bring about uncertainties and insecurity. These conflicts freeze their hopes. Kids need both parents to be able to follow through with their life project and bring it to a successful end. Some come to the adventure on earth with the purpose of cementing unions by mending broken pieces remaining from past grievances. The task of conciliation is a priority to all and there could never be too much effort or sacrifice, tolerance or understanding. If the price seems very high it is because the debt is equally large.

If, however, after all attempts have been made, the couple decides to separate it should do so in a civilized way, without aggressiveness and bitterness in order to diminish the pain inflicted on everyone, especially on the children.

Am I being too dramatic? Maybe... Does it sound like the end of the world? No... This is what we see all the time on the billboards modern society displays in these hard times. And if you ask me what I have to do with this, an elderly man in his seventies, in the last part of his life, I can give you my reasons.

A few years ago, on a trip to the United States, I was invited to lecture on the enigmas and perplexities of life. The reason for the invitation wasn't because I have ready-made solutions for human problems, but because I have stubbornly insisted on the need for society to embrace spirituality. Instead of seeing ourselves as spirits that are temporarily tied to a physical body, we assume the identity of this body and confuse it with our own individuality. We drag the spirit around as if it were a piece of junk and even think the spirit gets in the way when we try to accomplish the rubbish dictated by collective memory. "So what?" Why should we worry if it's almost time to go to this cosmic dimension you talk so much about?" you may insist. The answer is pure and simple dear ones. This won't be my last time here as it won't be yours either. When I come back in a new physical body for a new life I won't care what race I am, my color, nationality or social status. What I really want and ask God is that I have a father and a mother who love each other and who love me. I pray they give me the love and support I need until the time comes when I will have to follow my own footsteps. This is what I told the Americans that day.

If possible, I don't wish to find myself crying on some corner of the future because my mother couldn't stay with me and my father. I will need them every minute. I will need the love they feel for me as well as the love they feel for each other, for God and for life. I want them to talk to me about God, teach me again how to talk to Him and

CHAPTER 21.

see Him through my tears, feel His presence inside me in moments of cosmic harmony. How can I carry out this plan in a society that has forgotten Him, as much as it has forgotten itself because it cares only about immediate pleasures?

Chapter 22.
THERE IS NO NEED TO "BEND IT WHILE STILL A TWIG"

My book *A Memória e o Tempo (Memory and Time)* begins with the description made by a psychic of a procedure adopted in the first stages of initiation in Ancient Egypt. These tests which she not only describes but shares some secrets about were necessary for the initial evaluation of a candidate. Even if he passed those tests he would be subject to a careful and competent, although not obvious observation period for an unlimited amount of time. If he did pass these tests it would show that he had what it took to receive further knowledge although these aptitudes still weren't enough. Much more was required from the candidate who would undergo intensive learning under strict discipline.

Once this phase was accomplished he would be taken to a secret chamber where he would be subject to a memory regression session. He would then be guided and interrogated wisely and would dive deeply into the files of his integral memory in order to gather the necessary personal data that would be needed for the work program he would have ahead of him in his life on Earth. His masters and counselors would then know about predominant character traits, skills developed in previous lives, experiences he brought from the past, tendencies that needed to be corrected, knowledge and resources he would have to develop, tasks he would have to perform, preferences for this or that activity, commitments made in the spiritual world, personal relationships with those living in the flesh or as spirits and numerous other aspects.

With all these elements, it would be relatively easy to draw a clear picture of the person and the work schedule that would better fit into his commitments, both personal and collective.

How should we, who are common people living in times of ideological tumult in which the great values of life are being questioned and the knowledge of transcendental aspects has been lost or ignored, proceed to guide our children, grandchildren relatives and

CHAPTER 22.

friends in the best direction possible?

The truth is we do not have what it takes to perform this procedure in the same way they did in Egypt. And even if we did have what it takes (there are many people performing memory regressions at X Dollars or Reais per life) many people who are totally unprepared would be undergoing regressions guided by people who lack the right formation, out of mere curiosity.

As you noted, only the ones who had passed the necessary tests could undergo regressions in Egypt. Besides, such procedures had a noble and specific objective which was to draw a psychological, intellectual and ethical profile of the person so that he or she could develop the activities he or she had been programmed to perform here on Earth. Furthermore, such subjects would have shown to be able to know about events documented in their memories without being disturbed by such memories.

All this would be impossible nowadays because, although we master the regression technique itself, we lack the wonderful professionals and profoundly wise masters who were able to competently and respectfully handle the secret archives of the human mind.

On the other hand, the reader might be thinking that as our children usually are reborn bearing such a rich number of experiences and knowledge there is nothing we can or must do to help them. That is not true. There is much we can do to help them! And we must do it as we saw a few pages back.

If a spirit such as Beethoven's, Einstein's or DaVinci's happened to be born into your family would you just sit back feeling depressed and indifferent?

The truth is quite different. Firstly because we all go through longer or shorter periods in which we recapitulate and relearn as well as adapt and prepare. If Einstein is reborn he will again be a fretful baby whose mother will have to change his diapers, feed him and teach him how to walk, punish him when he misbehaves or even spank him if necessary. It is even possible that he will be prone to having nightmares for having contributed in such a decisive manner to the production of the first nuclear bombs.

Sometimes a Mozart is born who is extremely precocious and who is able, at only four or five years old *in the flesh* to overcome inhibitions and physical barriers to express the wonderful things he possesses deep down in his soul. In fact, few phenomena are so evident in expressing the existence of reincarnation as the magical ability of geniuses who are born already knowing everything they need to know. They are people who obviously carry a long and consolidated experience in the activity they have begun to develop either in the field of arts, sciences or any other. Did anyone have to teach Napoleon Bonaparte about military strategy? Didn't he know about it since he lived as Alexander the great or Julius Caesar? Would it be necessary to teach physics to Einstein if he was Democritus in Greece and talked about the atom. Would Rui Barbosa need lessons on politics if he had already lived the fruitful life of José Bonifacio de Andrada e Silva?

No matter the greatness or maturity of the spirit who is reborn among us, it will always require help in the period in which it is adjusting to its new body given him by its parents for its life on Earth. Humans have the longest childhood among animals. A dog who is three years old is an adult dog and the same happens to horses and cows. Birds need only a few weeks, insects, a few hours or a few days. A seven-year-old human being is still a helpless child who cannot find the food it would need to survive. With the growing demand for cultural development he (or she) will need to face the challenges of competing in a world which is becoming increasingly sophisticated and will only be ready for work and able to stand up to his peers at around 30 or even later.

While this happens there is a whole infrastructure to help, a logistics of physical, moral, psychological, cultural and social development. Even if the child is a genius it must be guided and corrected if it shows signs of aggressiveness, for example, or laziness and indifference and at the same time stimulated to develop inherent skills which are obvious. Parents must be attentive and study their children preferably without them noticing it. The best instrument for this search is conversation and communication. This is why we recommend talking to babies even if they are not able to answer us appropriately as we would like them to. At least they will know what we think about them and what the world around them is like. We will, in this way, be opening the channels of communication and will gain access to the small individual universe that everybody carries within themselves.

It is not true that a child is like soft clay and we can shape it into being what we want. There is a popular saying that states that "as the

CHAPTER 22.

twig is bent, so grows the tree". That is not exactly how things happen. This doesn't mean, however, that the child should be abandoned to her own wills, or conversely oppressed to a point in which there is no space for its personality to unfold.

Of course rebellious spirits, aggressive and prone to violence or cruelty must be corrected by means of serious but not exaggerated punishments. Parents must be firm. If a child is left to do whatever it wants, if parents indulge their children to all their wishes and think their wrong actions are cute they will raise misbehaved children and contribute to the consolidation of these negative tendencies which are hard to overcome.

If the reader allows me I can illustrate the theoretical aspects behind this set of interests by means of a story you might consider to be fiction. This episode impressed me so much that I wrote an article about it in English, published in the United States in 1965, I believe. I rewrote it many years later in Portuguese for publication in Brazil

Convinced that the composer Felix Mendelssohn-Bartholdy was the reincarnation of Wilhelm Friedemann Bach, one of Johann Sebastian's children, I established a parallel between their lives that occurred in Germany, 25 years apart from each other. Friedemann died in 1788 at 74, and had squandered the enormous talent he had inherited due to maladjustments and lack of discipline. Meanwhile Mendelssohn was born in 1809 and died in 1847 at the early age of 38.

In his short life as Mendelssohn it seems he had the specific task of restoring the magnificent music of Johann Sebastian Bach to the rightful honorable and outstanding place it greatly deserved. Wilhelm Friedemann had dealt with the great work of his father in a totally careless manner which made people forget his father's music very quickly. Much of the original written music was lost because of him and some were lost forever.

A generously gifted spirit such as this one who is at the same time, irresponsible, lazy, disorganized and rebellious will certainly need loving parents who are understanding and dedicated but who are also strict disciplinarians. This is what happened to Felix who was reborn to a wealthy, harmonious, intelligent and cultured family. His father Abraham and his mother Lea Salomon displayed a rare emotional balance between disciplinary strictness and love and understanding towards their children.

As he was submitted to this type of discipline and counted on his family's financial and emotional support, Felix was able to develop his vast talent with a safe precociousness of a person who already knew all of that.

I am not quite sure that he would have been able to accomplish so much in only 38 years of physical existence if it weren't for the marvelous group of spiritual friends in whose company he was reborn.

Discipline is therefore perfectly compatible with a mature, affectionate and creative relationship. It even seemed at times that the great Bach was supervising Felix's work and even wrote music through his hands as one can infer when listening to the beautiful introduction to his Third Symphony known as the *"Scottish"* written in honor of Mary Stuart.

I might add, again not asking readers to believe its veracity that the spirit of Willhem /Felix reincarnated once more, this time here in Brazil. The immense talent and sensitivity are still a part of his spirit, but, as he was not able to control the dispersive tendencies in his past life, he didn't develop such qualities this time around. He still squanders his talent due to the lack of mental discipline and wastes it in the same way Friedemann did.

Our spiritual progress is quite slow and although a spirit is always evolving there might be *relapses* when it hasn't really learned the spiritual lessons it has been taught. Instead of overcoming these mistakes by adding more discipline to our lives we choose to repeat the same mistakes.

So I won't say that "as the twig is bent, so grows the tree". We must water the twig with our kindness and keep it safe from weeds. There isn't the slightest doubt that in the same way that we are responsible for our children we must exercise our authority over them. It is very important that this authority be exercised with love and also with firmness. There is a time for saying *no* as there is a time for saying *yes*.

As seen before, there is a strong reason for the newly-incarnated spirit to go through a period in which it is more susceptible to guidance and counseling. I have met parents who regretted having been too condescending towards their children but I have never met any who regretted having been strict unless they have exceeded on their strictness.

CHAPTER 22.

As strange as it may seem, it is quite common for adults to praise their parents for the tight discipline they were submitted to in their childhood. Likewise, many adults complain about their parent's lack of interest in combating their negative tendencies. It is not by serving their every need that we show our children how much we love them. A perfect balance between respect, freedom and discipline is totally possible.

In this manner we will be helping them to develop the potential that was given to them by mother nature. The bent twig also needs support and understanding. One day it will realize from the shadow it projects on the ground that it isn't nice to be crooked. That is why next time it "reincarnates", through one of its seeds, it will make sure to grow upright and elegant, in the direction of the blue sky like all trees should.

God wishes us to be purified and redeemed but he doesn't rush us into this or exerts any kind of unbearable or deforming pressure. He prefers that we grow spiritually and physically according to our own personal rhythm and gives us the necessary space. Surely discipline is an indispensable ingredient in the *recipe* of life. Recently a very dear spirit told me that if God were excessively complacent towards us we would not have the chance to evolve.

To sum it up we can say that the twig should not be bent, it should be cultivated.

And speaking of God, which religion should we teach our children? Would it be better to make them nonbelievers so that they can decide for themselves?

We shall deal with this in the next chapter.

Chapter 23.
THE PRESENCE OF GOD

The readers who are atheists or disbelievers must be asking themselves: "But what does God have to do with all this?" Let me answer with another question. "What doesn't God have to do with all this and everything else in the Universe?"

Others who follow religions or sects might consider this to be a personal matter and that it is up to each one of us to decide. In principle we agree with this. The choice of following a religion or being agnostic represents a personal decision which must be respected. This does not mean, however we can't talk, in a polite and civilized way, about the many aspects involved.

The readers must not worry as it is not my intention to preach or to try to guide anyone into this or that sect. This is all part of a very complex context that results from a series of more or less imponderable aspects.

I believe that having a legitimate feeling towards religion is much more important than being just affiliated to this or that religion.

I believe (and hope) that at this point we have all learned that children are preexisting beings that pack a very wide religious experience in their spiritual baggage, in addition to other experiences. It is widely known that in remote times, stars, natural phenomena, animals, totem poles and even human beings were worshipped and adored. Greeks and Romans had Gods for everything and it would be foolish to say they were ignorant. It is exactly the opposite: Mythology is an extremely intelligent religious system that uses allegories and simple images to explain the many forces of nature or in other words to explain the need for a single God in the world we live in.

The truth is that the usual criteria used for our children to choose a religion (or not) are not very good. Either we let things take their own course or we force our children to follow "our" religion, i.e., the parent's religion or that of the person responsible. This is the reason why we see so many disoriented people when it comes to religious experience. The conflicts that result from arguments or differences regarding religion, a usually touchy subject, are very common.

For many, religion is just a habit, a social obligation, a secondary aspect of life, or as so many would say, a force that holds us back. (Are we cars or animals that need breaks or bridles?). In families who are used to a certain religion children are led to their parents' religion, what is understandable, and remain faithful to it for the rest of their lives without questioning if that is really what they want. I usually say they are *genetic* Catholics, atheists, Protestants as if they had inherited a specific gene from their parents, as many seem to believe.

It is true that religion should be taught to children in the same way and intensity as any other subjects. The spiritist institutions, for example, render an important service by teaching the gospel to children. I even urge parents to motivate their children to study different religions around their teens, even if they are irreligious or against any religious philosophy. It is not that this is essential to choosing the right religion for each of us, but it enables us to have a wider perspective of vital aspects regarding the understanding of life.

We carry ideological matrixes in our cultural baggage that are either consolidated or imprecisely defined. Past experiences are not decisive when it comes to choosing a religious or agnostic posture in each new life that begins on Earth. Not rarely, it is a choice made long before, that is, before the child is born, when it decides, due to respectable motivations, to go or is sent to a Catholic, Protestant, Jewish or Muslim family, for instance. It is not always that a child should automatically adopt the parents' religion without restrictions or difficulties. Parents should motivate children to consider other options. In this regard, we can sometimes find children, who from the moment they can express their thoughts start showing signs of rejection towards the religion of their parents, siblings, friends and relatives. This is usually a source of stress if common sense and tolerance are not exercised.

In fact, instead of bringing people together, especially because most cults express the same basic beliefs in different ways, paradoxically religions tend to lead to a large amount of intolerance, hate and bitterness which are hard to solve. Extreme religious followers believe that their religion is not only the best but the only one, outside which there can be no salvation. The worst part of this is that many religious followers rarely take the time to respect other people's faiths. What they actually do is to try to convince others that their truths are the only truths and to force them to adopt these truths as their own. Non-believers are themselves part of a cult who follow rituals and practice intolerance and fanaticism much the same way some religions do.

I hope the ideas in this book will help everyone have a more open and intelligent stance towards religion. After all, don't we all come from an unknown number of lives where we had so many different ways of facing religion? Who would say we have already worshipped the sun, the moon, stones, animals, objects, trees and a multitude of gods e goddesses? These are all experiences we gain, things we've learned which lead us to a safe nonstop process of arriving to the Truth.

Our relationship with the spirits in the course of many years over the time of our exchange with them has given us a privileged point of view of religion. What we see is the amazing amount of different religious experiences and the changes they go through over time. The moment we change our physical bodies and our social, historical, geographical and cultural environments we also replace our beliefs with other more rational ones. Unfortunately, many times what changes is external appearance, the priestly robes, the cults, rites and stance, gods and dogmas, formulas and hierarchic structures but we are still fanatic, dogmatic, intolerant, exclusivist and ambitious as well as interested in religious sects only to the extent that they are a springboard for personal success and the way to exercise power over others.

In our talks over the years we have met spirits who were so fanatical and intolerant in their fight against Christ that, as they belonged to priestly hierarchies at the time, they remained, centuries later, fanatical Christians, condemning those who were not Christians or who couldn't accept the form of Christianity being offered, to them.

Other spirits have told us that they made such commitments with the divine laws against religious power (Is there any other structure of thought that provides a stronger form of power than religion?) that they ended up by combating any idea, institution or concept pertaining to religion.

Let's therefore be realistic: children are people who carry a great amount of religious experience from former lives. It would be very

CHAPTER 23.

hard, after living so many different lives, not to have had some kind of religious involvement in time or space with the innumerable sects humankind has known. Many if not most of this experiences were disastrous and left scars which are difficult to remove as well as marks in the minds and bodies of many people. We do not speak here only of those who used religion badly or as an instrument of oppression, but also of those who suffered as a result of such mistakes and suffered unbearable oppression. This occurs because divine laws tend to work by alternating positions: the fanatic of today will eventually be a victim of others' fanaticism in the future.

In view of this worrisome picture, it seems unreal to expect children to accept religious concepts with ease or to make a calm, highly ethical and balanced decision regarding religion this time around. There were many serious imbalances, mistakes and even crimes committed in the name of the Lord which were disastrously justified as being manifestations of the love for God or Christ or for codes considered sacred, unique and untouchable.

Regarding this aspect, which is a touchy matter to many, it is my purpose to offer a personal testimony instead of telling stories about others.

You must remember that a few pages back I mentioned that I have had the opportunity to know about many of my previous lives. This is true and I am very grateful to my spiritual guides and mentors who taught me the things I've learned.

This experience has enabled me to form the basis of a beautiful and harmonic vision which has undoubtedly helped me shape a philosophy of life that is not only a one or two hour a week practice but a permanent posture. Religion is not an aspect of life. Life itself is religion in the sense that everything is within God, everything takes place within Him, all that happens is decided by the natural laws created by the Supreme Intelligence, everything flows towards Him and reflows from Him.

I know of lives lived in Egyptian temples, in mythological times, as in Greece, according to Hebrew teachings, as well as many centuries of catholic militancy and later the reformist movement of the XVI century. What can be learned from all this but that many things were added and many others subtracted in such a large religious experience? After so much suffering, so many mistakes and serious errors it is possible to distill purified concepts that sustain me further than just a belief and become strong convictions. This is it: we are immortal, indestructible, perfectible spirits and this is why we come and go from world to world, that is, the two sides of the same world. On one of these worlds we experiment a more dense life in the flesh with the limits it imposes; on the other, a more ethereal world, we live several other forms of life, as real as here on Earth, but where our senses are more refined, more subtle and where we are endowed with a greater sensibility.

When this life started I saw myself leaning naturally towards my mother's religion: Catholicism. She taught me how to pray, a wonderful and irreplaceable way of talking to God. She talked to me about God, about Christ and the Gospel. She taught me clean ethics using simple examples and words in a way that was easy to understand. As I would later find out (or maybe I had already known), the Truth is discrete, silent, transparent and so simple that some people don't even look at it. They believe it is an inexpressive and anonymous figure, lost in the crowd, who screams, wears flashy clothes showing off to passersby and even follows them or grabs at their clothes.

The decision my mother made about us was simple and practical. She took in the ten spirits generously, giving them bodies and guiding them in their first steps in the new life.

She remained a Catholic to the end, practicing her religion fervently and devotedly without however becoming a fanatic. (She taught us: "The obligations come before devotion") As long as we were under her guardianship we would remain Catholics. From then on it would be up to us to decide. I remember that I started feeling disenchanted about her religion when I was still under her care. I didn't feel attracted to the rituals, the vows and parallel obligations and much less to the reasoning that was taught to me. I began questioning them and the answers and explanations were not always to my liking. I am sure that she realized my disquiet and tried to insist that I followed the rituals of her religion which brought her so much consolation in her times of need, urging me to go to church or follow the sacraments so that my soul which she cared for so much would not be in danger.

She was, however, never forceful or imposing. It is easy to suppose that she would have preferred all her children to have been sheltered under the wings of her beloved Church but she never made

CHAPTER 23.

decisions for us, believing they were ours to be made after we became adults. She did try to lead us into her religion when we were kids because at that time we were unable to study and analyze the facts and decide which path to follow.

I am thankful for her common sense, balance, and intelligence. More than grateful I consider myself privileged to have been able to live with such a generous and calm although strict and decided spirit who was filled with a true sense of religiousness. I remember how important this was during the period between the time I questioned the doctrines of her religion and the time I had finally chosen my own doctrines which I already carried inside me, in the depths of my memory and would guide me in this existence.

It was a period of uncertainty, doubt and disquiet, as well as hopelessness and disenchantment. If that was not the way I should express myself as a human being in the universe I lived how should I do this?

Two important points remained inside me during this time of reformulation: the existence of God, which seemed more than obvious and indispensable in a clearly organic and harmonic universe, and the great admiration and respect for the majestic figure of Jesus and his basic philosophy which I read about in the bible.

When I received my first paycheck from a job I was being better paid for, I bought a copy of the Bible on July 31, 1939. I was nineteen years old. My mother, who was always attentive, warned me that it was a "protestant Bible" because it didn't include the tranquilizing "Nihil Obstat" or Imprimatur coming from the competent ecclesiastical authority. I tried to calm her, calling her attention to the fact that it was translated by father Antonio Pereira de Figueiredo but she noticed a few footnotes that she considered a bit suspicious. She did not, however, forbid me to read the book. I believe she trusted me and maybe the priest's translation. Besides there was a note saying:

"From the edition, approved in 1842 by Queen Mary II, in consultation with the Patriarch of Lisbon".

Deep down she knew, however, that this did not mean much as the text I had in hands *was taken* from the approved edition but it didn't mean *it was* the approved edition, even though it contained the pp (papal approval) inscription.

Whatever the case, this is the Bible I have used, among other newer ones, for more than fifty years.

Soon I began feeling a sort of connection with it. I believe today that it was at that time when I was trying to understand the meaning of these words that the barriers of time started falling and I could listen to Christ teaching me the beauty of His endless wisdom. I had spent so many lives listening and repeating those ideas that I knew them by heart. It was as if I had met old friends and rediscovered paths I had gone through long time ago, not knowing where or when.

To sum it up: Christ was once more inside me. Maybe he had always been there and I just didn't know it.

Many years later, a person who was deeply involved in the memories of his past told me that the concepts I used to reject in traditional Christianity were the ones my spirit disagreed with, in some still obscure way, and knew did not reflect Jesus' true ideas.

I don't expect everyone to believe my personal experience as a model to be adopted by all or by a few. I don't consider myself a redeemed, virtuous or perfect human being. I am well aware of my limitations and of how much I still need to go to reach a state of reasonable serenity. Besides, although the psychological mechanisms are the same or very similar in everyone, each one of us acts and reacts differently to stimuli coming to us from the outside. This complex movement is the result of a set of experiences which determine how mature or immature we really are. We are unique, individual beings, miniaturized universes, particles of consciousness, mere colorful dots that when joined together by the thousands and millions change the color of the community in which we live in and change the different times, historical, geographical and social contexts we are part of from time to time, life after life.

We end up finding our way as there is no other way but the way that leads to God. Nothing can be done if so many choose to be stuck in the mud or cross deserts and briar patches. Each person has the right and the responsibility to use their own freewill in regards to the situations that play out in front of us. After all, God is not in a hurry because he is beyond and above time and space. If one chooses to stubbornly and childishly go through life without him, as if this were possible, it will be a long and painful experience. We will find ourselves saying: "Oh Lord!" "How could so much time have been wasted!" "Why was there so much pointless suffering?"

CHAPTER 23.

This is where the ascent towards the light begins. The more generous hands are willing to help us, lighting our way, helping us up when we fall, encouraging us in solidarity and fraternal love, the easier and faster it will be.

This is what really matters, not this or that specific religion. We need to have God inside us and must be constantly aware of this presence. We begin to notice this for the first time in the hearts of generous mothers, before we realize He is within us too. If we can't see Him there, for whatever reason, we can be sure that it will be harder to find Him inside ourselves.

Chapter 24.
HOW TO TALK TO GOD

Somewhere in this book I suggested you should pray and if you don't know how to pray you must learn. As amazing as it may seem many people don't know how to do it. Prayer is a talk with God, a conversation needing no special formulas, rites or postures. The tone of the conversation is decided by the closeness you have with the one you are praying to. With God this relationship is very close. Who is the best person to know us, know about our problems, needs and potential? We must be very respectful towards Him. The composer and singer Gilberto Gil, in a beautiful song, tells us how the one who is praying should prepare to speak to God. Poets are very wise….

As did Francis, the young Bernardone, from Assisi.

When we lived in New York, in the fifties, we received a parchment from Malvina Dolabella with the prayer from St. Francis that she had put into verse and given to her friends. It read:

*Do give heed to me Lord, make me a channel of
Thy peace among men!*

That where there is injury, may I bring pardon.

*Where there is hate, may I leave in its place, Lord,
a smile of love!*

That where there is discord, may I bring harmony.

That where there is error, may I calmly bring the Truth! That where there is doubt, may I bring the faith that makes us love You!

*That where there is despair, and lack of faith,
may I bring the light of hope!*

*Where there is darkness may I bring light,
where there is sadness may I bring joy.*

And that that great day may come…

(and thanks to You, Lord, it will come!)

CHAPTER 24.

When may I not so much seek to be consoled as to console;

to be understood as to understand;

to know if I am loved as to love;

for it is in giving that we receive,

*the one who quenched others' thirst is
the one who drinks the most,*

it is when we forget ourselves that we find ourselves.

And forgiveness comes our way only... when we forgive too!

And I will wait for death smiling, convinced,

that only after death I will truly know Life!

There are many prayers both in the Old and in the New Testament as well. One of the oldest conversations with God is in Deuteronomy (9,26-29) where this prayer can be found:

"O Sovereign Lord, do not destroy your people, your own inheritance that you redeemed by your great power and brought out of Egypt with a mighty hand. Remember your servants Abraham, Isaac and Jacob. Overlook the stubbornness of this people, their wickedness and their sin. Otherwise, the country from which you brought us will say, 'Because the Lord was not able to take them into the land he had promised, and because they displeased him, he brought them out to put them to death in the desert.' But they are your people, your inheritance that you brought out by your great power and your outstretched arm."

This is a good example of an open-hearted conversation in which the one who prays recognizes the stubbornness of his people but asks that they be spared. After all, they are still those people who used to be slaves although they deserve to be strictly reprimanded. What would the Egyptians say if they were decimated?

Martin Luther used to pray looking out of an open window and contemplating the universe. In a letter to his friend Melanchton he wrote: *Oh, my Philip, it is prayer that governs the world, we get everything through it, we get up from our falls, we bear the incurable, we destroy evil, we conserve good."*

One day he found Melanchton feeling depressed and practically dead. He looked out the window and prayed like he never had, with the unshakable faith he possessed. After he did this he started talking to his friend, who began to recover in order to resume his fight. Later he would refer to that serious conversation he had had with God. "How wonderful that God had heard me", he explained. I filled his ears with all the promises for support and said he had to help me so that I could go on believing"

Christ himself prayed a lot during his long and hard meditations, as prayer is the invisible thread that ties us to God. Prayer is always possible in any place, moment or situation. It doesn't even need to be out loud, it can be just in our mind.

Children should be taught to pray from an early age, using their own words in their own way. The child can do this at any time of the day, either in the morning or at bedtime, before leaving the house or at mealtimes, when someone in the family is sick or just or to thank God for the privilege of being alive, in good health and for having the opportunity to learn and to reach spiritual evolution. No matter which faith the parents follow, there are always many opportunities for prayer. Each one should pray within the context of one's beliefs, be them Jewish, Muslim, Christian, Spiritist or Buddhist. One's religious faith is not what matters. Although many think they have their own private God, there is really only one God, our Father, and this makes us members of one big universal family. We are, therefore, all brothers and sisters.

When I wake up in the morning I ask God to bless the day ahead of me. When I open the windows, I look outside and mentally say: "Good morning, day!" When I am preparing to go out I ask God to help me deal with the people I might meet in the supermarket, at the bank, on the sidewalk, on the bus in the best way possible.

Many of us choose a certain hour of the day to pray for longer periods and to meditate. I prefer to pray at 6:00 pm when I am free from my daily chores. I make my own prayers and renew them from time to time so that they don't become automatic and mechanic. I want to be fully aware of what I am telling God or Christ.

Prayers, however, have some characteristics that we must know about. Sometimes we think prayers haven't been answered when they already have. Are you confused? Let me reword this: if the prayers had been answered according to the supplicant's requests the result might have been bad for them.

CHAPTER 24.

Furthermore prayers should not be wasted. God is not at our disposal to gratify all our whims. They are a way to make us stronger in the face of difficulties, not a means of winning the lottery or removing obstacles in our path. Firstly because we ourselves created these obstacles and facing these difficulties is the way we become stronger and learn what we need to.

It might appear to the reader that I am preaching. This isn't true. I am speaking of an undeniable reality. Outside religion, prayer has been researched scientifically and the findings have been very surprising. Dr. Franklin Loehrs' careful work in The United States has shown the power of prayer over the growth of plants, for instance, as he describes in his book *"The power of prayer on plants"* The results could be measured when comparing two groups of the same kind of plant which were planted and treated in the same manner. Both groups of plants received water, soil and light although one of the groups received prayers as well, prayers to the water and to the plants themselves. It was soon possible to see which plants were receiving the prayers as they were healthier, stronger and bigger.

If the reader is interested I recommend chapter 40 – "The power of prayer over plants" on pages 143 to 145, from the book "De Kennedy ao homem artificial" (From Kennedy to the artificial man). This book gathers articles that were written in the 60's by Luciano dos Anjos and I during three years for the Diário de Notícias, a very well-read and traditional newspaper in Rio de Janeiro no longer in circulation. One of these articles, published on November 29, 1968 is about prayer (pages 100-102). I will use it to make additional remarks.

From my perspective there are two kinds of people who don't pray: those who don't know how and those who don't want to. This talk is aimed preferably at the first group without excluding the other because both are neglecting to have an exchange with the supreme energy

that supports the universe. We hope that we have reached those who don't know how to pray and well as the indifferent ones. We might even add a third group: those who pray mechanically and repeat the same emotionally empty formulas endlessly. For what is prayer if there is no sentiment?

Many still don't know that the power of a prayer lies not in the number of times we repeat it but in the feelings of our spirit while saying it. Those who use repetitive formulas don't know what to tell God if these formulas no longer work.

The entries in the Encyclopedia Britannica describing prayer I looked up are very technical. They divide it into three groups as to whom the supplicant is praying to: one superior, equivalent or inferior to him in his point of view. To God one should pray in humbleness and trust. To a saint one proposes a bargain or makes a promise on more or less the following terms: "Do this for me and I promise to do that." The third type, still according to the Brittanica, is literally a threat: "Do this or I'll break your neck."

It is unnecessary to say that the two latter forms of "prayer" are out of the question here. As I've said before, memorized, readymade prayers are not my favorite either. If prayer is a direct understanding between a human being and God or a superior being whom we trust, Christ, for example, it is only necessary to open one's heart and let it talk in a loyal, frank, respectful and quiet way. There is no need to use difficult words or sophisticated expressions which usually sound fake. They end up sounding like a political speech instead of a prayer. Don't be ashamed of your language when talking to God, He will understand you perfectly, and the simpler and humbler the better because it is the feeling behind it that counts and not the "pretty words".

Jesus didn't worry about teaching us specific prayers. The only one he left in his words was the "Our Father". What else did he say? He said that when we had to pray we should enter a room and secretly address God. He mentioned the value of the simple man's humble and sincere prayer and the ineffectiveness of the hypocritical Pharisee's pompous prayer.

He also said we had to knock so that doors could be opened to us. Whether we get what we want or not is a different story. Not always is what we ask for good for our spirit. Professor Rivail's instructors told us that Christ has taught us that God will not give us stone if we ask for bread, but as a caring father he will refuse to give his children what is bad for them.

It is important to stress that children should learn how to pray early on in the same way that they are taught to brush their teeth, keep clean and behave. The habits acquired early on will remain throughout one's life and show what kind of childhood one had. As in many other aspects of family life learning through examples is the most efficient form of learning. The child should leave home for the first time prepared to resist the inevitable aspects of "unlearning" they face in the street, in school, on the bus or train.

If one of the parents or both of them is in the habit of praying children will get used to doing this. The best way is to do this on a regular basis. Many families read the Bible at home. The family gets together once a week, preferably in the evening, to pray, read a page and comment on it. Half an hour is enough. If you are not Christian, pray with the Torah, the Coran, or the teachings of whatever master you follow. Stimulate the children to participate and comment on the subjects mentioned.

By the way the power of learning through examples is decisive in so many other areas of life, as we have seen, not only in religion. I was raised in a time in which bad words were, to say the least, rude and inelegant and pronounced only by those with no manners. We would not use this kind of language around our family. My brothers and I never used swear words because my parents didn't. We continued this tradition in the family my wife and I began. None of us use swear words although many people use it on the streets, in the movies, on TV and in written texts. I accept being called "square" or puritanical without any embarrassment when it comes to cursing. It always shocks me to hear a child or a woman using such language. I still believe the mouth becomes dirty when the time to talk to God comes and I have no desire of changing my way of seeing this.

I have no miraculous, ready-made prayers to teach. Every one of us has their own unique, private way of expressing themselves. I like "Our Father" of course. I have even made a long lecture on it because there are many things to be learned from it. For example:

Have you noticed that the only material request in it is that of bread? And more, the daily bread, not a mountain of bread. I also like St. Francis of Assisi's prayer and although it shouldn't be endlessly repeated I enjoy the prayer made by a spirit who called himself Agar and written by the dear Chico Xavier.

"Father of infinite kindness; help us keep our hearts on the road you have chosen for us. Instill in us the desire to help those around us, sharing with them the little we have so that happiness multiplies among us. Give us the strength to fight for our rehabilitation, in the work circles we were sent to by your wise wishes. Help us fight our

own weaknesses so that we don't fall into darkness as victims of violence. Oh lord, don't let happiness make us weaker and do not allow the pain to suffocate us. Teach us how to recognize your kindness in all the good things that happen to us. In days of agony make us look at your light through our tears and in times of comfort help us to share your blessings with our peers. Make us accept suffering, have patience at work and get help for difficult tasks. Give us, above all, the grace of understanding your will, whatever it may be, wherever we are so that we know how to serve in your name and so that we are children worthy of your infinite love. Amen.

Isn't this a beautiful prayer? I love the words "look at your light through our tears" and

"sharing with them the little we have so that happiness multiplies among us."

A prayer such as this one has no religious denomination. It is good for everyone, even for non-believers in a moment of difficulty. About these, my mother used to say that people remember Saint Barbara only when there is lightning.

Prayer is never something boring or a daily sacrifice we must make. It is that special moment we tap our spiritual energy into the great reservoir of cosmic energy.

Chapter 25.
THE PS THAT BECAME A CHAPTER

I was thinking about adding some notes to the previous chapter when I realized that these notes were not sufficient to cover the subject which deserved a chapter of its own. So, here it is.

As I mentioned before, I became unhappy with the religious structure provided to me in my childhood from an early age. It was not easy to have rejected these values. It was good while it lasted because in everything I saw the soothing image of my mother teaching us and making observations. In fact there was such a strong connection that at one point I seriously considered dedicating myself to a religious life. Strange as it may seem, my classmates nicknamed me "Vicar" as I was a recluse and did not act as others of my age did. I refused to use profanity as I do up to this day. Everybody knew I disliked distasteful jokes or conversations which embarrassed me. This continues to date.

Suddenly I saw myself without a specific religion and that bothered me and disenchanted me in a certain way. Many years later I would read in Silver Birch, the wise spiritual guide of Maurice Barbanell, that we, human beings, worry too much about labels. Similarly Saint-Exupery mentions in "The Little Prince" that people are very worried about numbers. This is true for when people meet each other they quickly want to know how old the person is, how much money he or she earns a month, how much his or her home is worth, how many kids he or she has and things like that.

At that time, however, I still didn't know that labels weren't important at all. They can make it easier to identify someone but are not useful if they don't represent a belief. Whether I wanted to or not, I think this bothered me. The label "Catholic" was no longer mine to use and I had no other label to replace it with.

For some unknown reason I wasn't keen to the label "protestant" either. I didn't consider being Muslim or Buddhist. I completely rejected being an atheist and being a spiritist didn't occur to me especially because of all I had heard and read about the "dangers" of this "sect" or "heresy" sponsored mainly by the devil which represented a surefire way to guide a poor helpless and unguarded soul straight to hell.

My quest continued. I needed a label but where could I find one and how could I know if it was the right one to replace the old one I had refused?

At the same time, however, I "knew" there was a label waiting for me somewhere which I was yet to find. It was thus a matter of time and patience before I found what I was looking for.

In the meantime I avidly read the Bible returning to the points that interested me, especially the epistles of St. Paul which I loved although some of its aspects and teachings seemed obscure and incomprehensible to me. As all of this should make sense I knew I needed a sort of key with which I could open doors and safes which held treasures of knowledge.

Today I am able to see that I was a Christian, but in a sense that differed from the conventional Christianity that was offered me. Besides, religious authorities whom I heard and read for a long time decreed that in order to be a Christian and go straight to heaven one had to belong to the church they represented. I looked up the word Christian in the dictionary and it said the same thing: A Christian is a baptized individual who professes Christianity. I had been baptized, it's true, but I honestly could not say that I *professed* Christianity.

I spent many years looking for the right label that would define me. I considered myself a Christian and had a label but it had no value for others who did not recognize me as one.

Only when I was around 35 did I start examining seriously the doctrine the spirits had conveyed to Allan Kardec. I asked a personal friend of mine who was a specialist on the subject to give me some books about it. I followed strictly the *prescription* he had made on a small piece of paper where he had written the names of some authors whom he trusted.

It was not difficult to accept the ideas contained in those books. On the contrary, I had the impression that I had finally found the way I was destined to follow. It was very strange at that time to realize that these apparently new teachings weren't new to me. It seemed these things had been kept in some unconscious drawer of my mind

CHAPTER 25.

and I was just discovering what was in it. To sum it up I was a spiritist and didn't know it.

There was still one problem left to solve. My mother remained a devout, practicing Catholic. She remained faithful to her beliefs and was very suspicious of everything regarding spirits and spiritism as she had been repeatedly taught that these were things of the devil. Because she was never a fanatic she was able to live peacefully with relatives and acquaintances that chose to follow spiritism.

I don't know if she found out when she was still alive that I had joined the "heretics". If she did know she must have constantly prayed and feared for the fate of my soul. Her birthday gift, which had no gold or silver, as Peter would say, was to attend a mass and observe communion for me. I am sure that the pureness of her faith and the strength of her prayers helped us all to find the right paths in life. She seemed to be close to God because she had had conversations with Him all her life in the silence of her meditation practice or when she was praying at a sick child's bed.

I didn't want to and couldn't hurt her feelings. I kept my beliefs hidden from her because after all our God was the same as well as our Gospel, our Christ whom we both loved, each one in one's own way.

I had something to solve at the time, though. I wanted to write about the things that were in my mind. I wanted to share some of the ideas that shaped my aspirations. More than this, I was beginning to understand, by way of the Gospel and epistles, matters I believed to be obscure or impossible to understand.

On December 1956, when I was 36, I began timidly and amateurishly writing for the *"Reformador"* newspaper. I worked there for 24 years. As I had a lot of respect for my mother's faith I signed my first articles with only my initials which were the same as hers: H.C.M.

One day, however, I thought it was my duty to write her an open letter explaining why and when I had become a spiritist. This small testimony was called "Letter to a Catholic Mother" as can be found in the *"Reformador"* issue of May, 1961. I signed it João (from João Marcus, a pseudonym I started using soon after and that I would continue using even after I started signing my real name.

Years later she had left to the spiritual world, Divaldo Pereira Franco, my dear friend and medium from Bahia gave me a message he was not quite able to understand but reproduced faithfully. A lady, whose appearance he described, came to him and said she had read my letter and to tell João Marcus that she was deeply touched by it and said thank you.

"Who is João Marcus?", he asked.

I explained everything as best as I could, given the profundity of that moment.

She would still send me many messages and would several times show herself through clairvoyance to mediums whom I trusted.

Once, when I was going through a more difficult period and was feeling tormented she decided to communicate through letters written by mediums, via written texts.

My mother was known to her family members to write in a beautiful and simple way.. She had a very clear, personal and unsophisticated handwriting that reflected her style and her own way of life.

She continued her writing in the afterlife. The letters had the same beauty, the same fluent style, the same underlying calm emotions and the same easygoingness one would use in conversation.

Having removed the personal touches, here is part of what she wrote to me in that document:

"A mother's love is like a fountain that produces love continuously in an endless flow that is lost through all eternity. A mother cries her children's tears when she no longer cries her own."

"(…) I have never liked to talk too much or to write. You know I have never felt comfortable with words. In a certain way they have always intimidated me. Now I know that it was the fear my spirit had of deviating from the work I had to perform."

"When I was alone in silence I talked to Jesus, trying to understand his desires and obey his words. Now I know he was not God. But now, I also feel him closer to my heart and more real. However, I had no difficulty in finding myself in this new reality because my faith, although simple and unadorned, was sincere and deep. Now I am learning that to Jesus there are no saints or sinners,

CHAPTER 25.

just siblings on their way to heaven"

"Finding family members and friends living a common life was undoubtedly a surprise to me as I didn't expect heaven to be real. But I was extremely happy to know that hell and the devil are words that were made up by the lazy who chose to settle for the least effort."

"I thank you, my son, for being who you are. I thank you for having followed the beliefs of your faith despite your respect and love for me. Today I see how much wiser it would have been if, although quite old physically, I would have listened to the melody of the new faith that flowed from your heart. But we learn lessons everyday and I will continue learning from you in the same way you learned from me. Today I am the one who wants to finish my lessons quickly and get to the end of the book, which in fact doesn't exist, because the Book of Life unfolds in the pages of the infinity.

"Don't give up, son. If I wasn't able to give you much, at least I gave you the example of tenacity and perseverance, trusting in life and believing in my duties."

"We are all working and studying. Here we learn that there is no separation of families and no social conventions. Everyone feels the same in terms of their desires, hopes and pains. Keep going. Don't allow adversity to divert you from your path towards your duties with Christ and with your faith. You know better than I what it's worth. Go on my son. This is your mother asking you this. Your heart is kept in my heart."

(….) This letter is getting very long and you might be asking how your mother who never spoke much can be saying so much. I thank Jesus for this opportunity and pray that the Lord may hold you in his lap and cradle your weary head in His hands encouraging you in his peace.

I close this letter with all the love in my humble heart, Helena, your mother."

This is a moving and beautiful document. I know there are many who don't believe in these radical posthumous conversions of people who used to be Catholic and are now using irony to describe it. Irony, however is not reasoning. The firm and clear witness of the fact is beyond reasoning. It is not that the people who die become *spiritists,* what happens is that they find out they are *spirits.* They realize they were prisoners of a mortal physical body. The only difference is that spiritists already knew they were *spirits* when they were in the flesh. There is no other difference because we are all siblings, although not always friends and we are all programmed to reach the same destiny of happiness and harmony.

I have one more thing to say about my mother's letter. Although she was always tired of taking care of the house and of raising ten children we all started school already knowing how to read, write and count. Although I was not especially brilliant I was able to learn everything with great ease. For me it was boring to stop at every lesson until she found the time to study with me. This is why I asked to be excused from this activity mainly because I was already reading the last pages of the *"Cartilha de infância"* (Spelling book for children) by Thomaz Galhardo. This is why she wrote: Now I am the one who wishes to finish my lessons quickly and get to the end of the book(…) And as follows, the newly learned lesson : "the book of Life unfolds in the pages of the infinity.

From this personal testimony which illustrates the problem of a child's religious education there remains only one doubt I leave to the reader as I myself have not been able to solve it. Who is more thankful to whom? My mother who now thanks me for what I couldn't do or didn't know how to do for her, or myself, for everything she did for me although she believes she couldn't give me much more than the wonderful example of her faith? For isn't this the "much" and the "everything" she gave me?

Chapter 26.
FROM THE SOLID STATE TO THE GAS STATE

Much has been said about life and we must also talk about death, which is a different kind of life and isn't that different from life as we know it in many respects.

As we grow up, get married and grow old people we love start dying. I have mentioned my mother's death. She died when I already knew that our separation would be temporary, although it might take a few years, as I too like everyone else was reborn programmed to return to the spiritual dimension I came from. Life here is just a learning and working stage which is part of an evolutionary cycle much the same way there are different grades in school. We take tests and pass them, oral and written tests, college entrance exams, do masters and doctorates, moving ahead and overcoming new hurdles. One day we will "graduate" and we will receive a kind of cosmic dimension diploma. When this happens we will never have to return to the so called "valley of tears". We will, around this time have become free from what the oriental mystics call "the wheel of reincarnation".

The very long path on which we learn about life will still go on but we will no longer need a limiting physical body from time to time.

In a letter to Godofredo Rangel ("A barca de Gleyre"[1]), a dear friend with whom he exchanged many letters, Monteiro Lobato said that death is just a change in state from the solid state to the gas state.

This doesn't mean however that we shouldn't feel bad about losing relatives and friends or simple acquaintances. Goodbyes are always emotional, whether it is a child who is going away for vacation or the death of a loved one. We miss the child who started a new job, the daughter who got married, the brother who went to live somewhere else far away and even a colleague and good friend who was transferred to a different branch of the company.

---
[1] By Monteiro Lobato (NR)

It is only natural and understanding that we feel sad when a person who is part of our spiritual group dies, especially those we love, for their virtues or for the closeness we have with them, whether they are relatives or not.

The loss of a child is extremely painful, no matter its age or how it died and its life in the flesh was interrupted. During the first moments of pain, we barely notice others' words of consolation, kindness and solidarity.

Everything seems hopeless. The loss seems permanent, the pain inconsolable and unbearable. It is useless to wish someone to magically stop crying and to start smiling under such emotional circumstances. We need time to grieve and to resume our life in such sadness. There are others around who need us, chores that need to be done, activities which cannot be interrupted. Life has no periods, only commas, semicolons, ellipsis points, exclamation marks, question marks and many hyphens. We aren't islands, as we said before, but particles of one continent, or if you wish, photons, more or less shiny, that are part of one and only light focus, for we live and move in God as our dear Paulo de Tarso said in such a perfect way.

There are no losses. No one dies forever. No one "disappears", no one is sent to a final destination after death. If love joined us to other human beings with whom we lived here, these bonds continue after we die in a sometimes even stronger way. I never agree with a suffering spirit who tells me that someone *loved* him or that he *loved* someone.

As Mario de Andrade used to say, "love is an intransitive verb." I also believe it is defective as it has no past form, only present and future. Who has loved once, will continue loving if it is really love and not passion.

In the beautiful poem in chapter 13 of his *First Epistle to the Corinthians,* Paul used the Greek word ***agape*** in his essay about the excellence of charity. According to the commentators of the *Jerusalem Bible*, ***agape*** is unconditional, self-sacrificing, active, volitional, and thoughtful love. It is such a pure and beautiful fraternal love that translators preferred to translate the word ***agape*** into ***charity.*** So, from versicle 4 on in that text, one should read *love* instead of *charity*.

Love is patient, love is kind. It does not envy, it does not boast, it is not proud.

CHAPTER 26.

It is not ambitious, it is not self-seeking, it is not easily angered. Love does not delight in evil but rejoices with the truth. It always forgives, always believes, always hopes, always suffers. *Love never ends.*

And how could it end if it is from the essence of God itself?

This is why love survives with the spirit, as it never dies, just changes states, as Lobato used to say.

The person who left to the other side of life does not leave forever those who stayed behind; it just went somewhat before for a reason that we will one day learn. When our time comes to leave, those who left before us, if they really loved us, will be there waiting for us with the same happy smile, the same friendly hug, the same generous heart. It is just a matter of time and patience, acceptance and serenity.

The Divine Laws are strict when it comes to rebelliousness, impatience, or lack of acceptance of what is prescribed to us. It is extremely hard for a couple, such as some friends of mine, to sit back and watch the inevitable departure of their only son, one who was so handsome, intelligent, full of life and hope, who had just graduated from college and was preparing himself for a promising future. Even when knowing the important aspects of the mechanisms of the Divine Law it is true that many have suffered for long periods of time before they were able to resume their lives from that difficult moment when the silence of separation took over. They knew, however, that we are all immortal spirits and that we are here temporarily so they were able to accept the determinations of the Law as they know they are not punitive but remedial.

Some forgotten situation in the past which remains in the global memory of spirits will certainly explain what caused all that pain.

Besides, as said before, our children are first God's children and God entrusts them to us temporarily. We don't own them, they aren't our private property and they can't be ours as if we had signed a contract. They are partners on the road we travel on for some time until they leave, suddenly, to wait for us in the near future.

Luther cried and prayed at his teenage daughter Magdalena's bedside:

"Lord", he said. I love her so much but if it is your will to take her I agree. I would very much like to keep her here with me. But

Lord let your will prevail. Nothing better could ever happen to her."

He then turned to the dying girl and started talking to her:

"My dear Magdalena, you would like to stay with me, wouldn't you? Are you willing to go to your Father who is in heaven?"

"Yes father", she answered. "I will do whatever He thinks is best for me."

"Yes, my dear daughter" he said. "You also have a father in Heaven and you are going to be with him".

But the pain was there too, crushing the consolation of his faith and he turned to his friends and said:

"The spirit is strong, but the flesh is weak. I love her so much!"

Melanchton said that "the love of parents for their children is the image of divine love. If the love of God for human beings is as big as the one parents have for their children then one could say this love is like a flame."

When the girl finally passed away at 9:00 am the next morning, Luther said in tears:

"I am so happy in spirit but so sad in the flesh. Poor me! The flesh refuses to agree. Separation is very painful. Isn't it wonderful to know that after suffering so much she is now in peace in an excellent place?"

Even though we know life goes on after death it is impossible to ignore the pain, just flip a switch and turn off one's feelings. The spirit believes and wants it but as Luther said, the flesh is weak and disagrees and the image seen through the flesh is blurred with tears.

I remember having been in this situation many times and if I live longer I will have to face this reality again. One of these times was when my grandmother died.

She was quite old, the poor darling and felt uncertain in her stride but was lucid and participating. Whenever she came to visit us after she said hello to us she would go straight to her quiet and very clean room. She usually carried something she was sewing in her hands and held it very close to her eyes as she had never had to wear glasses.

I would ask her for her blessing, kissing her thin and elegant hand

CHAPTER 26.

and spend a long time talking to her. I could see how happy she was to be with me and to know I loved her.

I had no idea what a void her departure would leave inside of me. I helped taking her light and tired body to the cemetery and stayed a little longer after everyone else had left. I wanted to pray silently for her. But the prayer came under the form of tears that run down my face, tears shed by the deep feeling I already had of how much I would miss her. They didn't have though, the bitter taste of revolt. As Luther said, God wanted her back and who was I to say no?

After that moment I left feeling confident and calm. She was in good hands. "in the hands of God, in his right hand", as Anthero de Quental had written.

There are, therefore, no words of consolation for those who lose their loved ones, only words of solidarity and fraternal kindness. Consolation will come later when we understand and *accept* death for what it really is – a short separation, not more than this.

An idea that is not always recognized might bring some comfort in this period of mourning. If the ones who remain are desperate and cannot be comforted they will be like poisoned thorns in the heart of the departed. After-death testimonies all agree on this point. As much as controlled pain is a sign of love, despair which is close to rebelliousness causes extreme distress to those who have left. They are tears that are similar to chains that bond the spirits to their sadness and frustrations on earth instead of sending them a message of consolation. These tears create obstacles that make their journeys more difficult.

We sometimes find an exaggerated bond that almost seems like an ownership as if God had no right to determine, through the infallible mechanism of his laws, the best way to guide us on our evolutionary scripts. It's as if the desperate parents complained to God for having had the "audacity" of separating them from their sons or daughters. After all, they might think: she is *my* daughter, he is *my* son!

Others wish to know at all costs about the deceased relative once they find out (and not very well) about the possibility of an exchange with spirits. If they aren't able to do this or if they are not convinced of what they were told they double their complaints and become revolted against God and against religion in general which, as they see it, hasn't helped them at all in their moments of pain.

However, this is not the way things happen. As our dear Chico Xavier says, the connection with the other world only works one way, from there to here, and if it is possible and permitted. We can't demand that our "dead" speak to us any time we want to as we would when using long distance calls. The spiritual world has its own guidelines and laws which must be respected.

Xavier's work in the last phase of his long, prolific life focused on this aspect of life – the words of consolation. There are many testimonials of people, especially young people, chiefly those who died in car accidents. It is not enough to join the uncomforted mother and Xavier so that he can summon the spirit of the dead son and make him talk immediately when requested.

There is a discipline to be followed, a system of priorities and possibilities that should be observed. It is impossible to make demands, ask for attention, ignore barriers or impose conditions. The testimonials might come, when possible, following rules that we know nothing about, in a context we ignore in terms of its details and disciplines.

In many cases we have to be content in believing that the person is still alive, conscious and happy (or unhappy), according to his or her own spiritual conditions. We cannot make this situation of uneasiness worse and should not disturb the spirit's tranquility with rebellious and uncontrolled despair. It is infinitely more intelligent and human to pray for his or her soul, peacefully although there is no doubt this person is greatly missed.

Prayer calms the soul of those who pray as well as soothes those receiving its good vibrations. The deceased spirits want us to go ahead with our lives, being happy with practicing good deeds and loving our neighbors so that one day we can all meet again without feeling like we own others.

Nobody belongs to anybody because we all belong to God. Today's son might have been the father or brother in a past life or in a life which is still in the unknown future.

There are no separations for those who love each other. There are separations for those who believe they own others just because they provided them with a physical body to live for a short time on earth.

This is why, Edgard Cayce, the American psychic said that "love is not possessive, it just is."

Chapter 27.
"SEE YOU"

Dear readers the time has come for us to say goodbye, at least for some time. One never knows when we will meet again as we have learned that life never ends.

The intention of this book was not to solve all the possible problems of this aspect of life which is so broad and complex or to answer all the questions there are because it would be impossible to know all the answers. I just tried to share some thoughts about the childhood of human beings on Earth which we still know so little about.

As we have seen we still have a lot to unlearn and to learn about this subject. We can only put new furniture into our house (our mind) if we get rid of old furniture which we no longer need. But renovation is not only about discarding everything we had and buying brand new things. In some aspects all we need to do is rearrange or restore some of the old pieces that might still be of use.

We know, for example, from old beliefs, that the human being possesses a soul and that this soul is immortal or at least that it survives the death of the body it has on Earth. Well, there is, however, a large piece of furniture obstructing the living room in terms of one of its most important points - that this soul is created in the moment of conception or birth when, in fact, it already existed before in other lives and certainly will return many times for future existences in the flesh.

The concept of personal responsibility that we all have for the acts we practice can and must be a part of our intellectual furniture but it should be renewed. We are not condemned without pardon for the mistakes we make in our lives. As also we don't go straight to heaven even if have lived an ideal life from the human point of view. This is so because heaven itself can only continue to serve us if it goes through quite some remodeling. Divine laws constantly give us opportunities to recover. If Christ asked us to pardon seventy times seven how many times would God pardon us? The answer is: always.

It so happens that the concept of pardon also needs updating and upholstering as forgiveness is not magically forgetting a mistake. Magic is an illusion and the laws are realistic and objective. The pardon granted us by the Divine laws expresses itself in the opportunity to make the same mistakes again. Until we learn.

Dying is no tragedy and is almost always – if the person lived a good although limited life – a moment to become free and to reunite with unforgotten loved ones. Being born is what is somewhat of a problem since we bring programs and tasks to perform, obligations and commitments we are not always able to perform adequately and that sometimes we even complicate.

There is a great exchange between the living and the dead, between those living in the flesh and in the afterworld; a relationship that is much more active and intense than we could ever suspect and which we are not consciously aware of. People who have special abilities can serve as intermediaries between the two sides of life, showing us important aspects of what awaits us on the other side. It is always important to remember, however, that everything is life, both in this side and in the other. And that the "dead" are people, like us.

Children are people too. They are adults with a lot of experience who sometimes have a greater intellectual capacity and a greater cultural baggage than many of us. The difficulty they experiment in the beginning of their lives in the flesh is just that of learning how to deal with their little body machine on Earth which is only "ready" to work full force in their teens and usually only in the adult phase.

The limitations a child has are a result of the weakness of its body, not of its spirit. Many years are needed to adapt to this body and to reach the time when it can respond to the commands given by the mind that was joined to that body in the beginning of pregnancy. It is a slow and difficult learning process as many complexities are involved. It must learn how to adapt to its environment, develop an adequate communication system and develop culturally. It must recover physical and mental skills as well as the techniques of living with those around it.

The mechanisms of life are subtle and intelligent. While the physical body is being formed the repetition of secular conquests becomes apparent. It's as if the body studied, in about nine months, all the thousands of years of its phylogenetic experience since, as

CHAPTER 27.

Lyall Watson would say, life has learned to duplicate itself, that is, to reproduce itself.

I hope Watson doesn't get angry at me if I try to say this in a different way. It wasn't life that learned the process of renovation. Life taught human beings this process as it had plans for us we couldn't even imagine as we didn't even have imagination.

It also seems that the spirit tries to recapitulate its evolutionary process. Although it comes to a life in the flesh with all of its potential preserved and ready to interact with the environment, this knowledge and past experience are kept in a closed although accessible compartment. It needs an opportunity, a new beginning as if it had just been created, a simple and ignorant being, as our instructors would say in a state of purity and innocence usually attributed to children.

This is maybe why Jesus told his disciples, *"Let the little children come to me, and do not hinder them, for the kingdom of God belongs to such as these."* When it regresses to its spiritual childhood the spirit is usually simple, pure, naïve, spontaneous and authentic. It is very open to others' influence whether this influence is a good or a bad one.

Whether the child is influenced negatively or positively will depend on the behavioral matrixes the child brings with it from its former spiritual lives. We will always be open, to a greater or lesser extent to the influence of others but in no other phase is this predisposition as obvious as in childhood.

That is why parents, tutors, guidance counselors, educators have such a big responsibility towards children who can be stimulated to give an important step forward and to develop their faculties of the mind and potentials they already carry within themselves. Or, otherwise, they can stop in time or repeat situations that could have been overcome if they had been taught to live adequately with the right motivations and to follow the healthy path towards personal realization as a spirit with a luminous and wide perspective in the evolutionary process.

The presence of God is extremely important in all of this not as a simple theological concept or the *need* to believe and the convenience of belonging to this or that religion, but as a *conviction*, as a conducting element, the essence in itself of the process of life.

We don't necessarily have to be Christian, Muslim, Buddhist or Jewish to "save" our souls, find the houris in heaven, reach nirvana or rest in the bosom of Abraham. All of these are imperfect images and inadequate ways of showing a unique reality – that of spiritual perfection which Jesus defined as being the realization of the Kingdom of God within us all.

The holy books of all religions contain principles that can be observed, but it is not just by reading these books as if they were mere philosophical treaties or by following a series of rituals and postures that we will reach the stage of perfection which awaits us. It is by *really* practicing the simple laws of brotherly love, for the universe is one only and immense brotherhood divided into innumerable communities of intelligent beings spread out all over the cosmos from galaxy to galaxy.

We would then have many questions to ask. The beautiful adventure of life presents a series of aspects and facets. One of these aspects is exactly the stimulating effort of the search. A spirit friend who is very intelligent and knowledgeable confessed to me that far from feeling frustrated by all he still ignored about the wonders of life, he felt fascinated when realizing all the beauties he still had to learn in the huge books of infinity. Like us here, he had more questions than answers in his mind. Living will never be a routine task.

Hence, it was not our purpose to teach how children are, how they should be guided or how they can be misguided by our carelessness. Our purpose was to question ourselves, exchange ideas, evoke the sweet anxiety to learn more, to decipher other enigmas of life, enlarging the space for learning, where the immense supply of future knowledge lies. Thus we conquer pacifically the unknown territory of ignorance.

If I may ask you something, dear reader, is that you keep thinking, questioning things and meditating. If we know how to ask the right questions truly willing to learn with the right amount of humbleness, life will answer us. God, who is inside us will answer with the light pushing away the shadows. This is how we are able to see the vast and beautiful world He made for us which we couldn't see precisely because there was a shadow upon us and not upon the world.

As we are all in this journey together and life is a way of travelling and not a station as someone said, it is likely that we will meet somewhere during this trip. Or it might even be that we have already met somewhere in the past.

So...*I'll see you!*

***

PS: I decided not to include some subjects in this book so that it wouldn't be too long and also because they have been described elsewhere in my other books and in those of others. I would like to mention four of these aspects: education, family, sexuality and drugs. All of these have a lot to do with the theme of this book. If the reader is interested I recommend the book written by my dear friend and colleague Deolindo Amorim, *O espiritismo e os problemas humanos* (Spiritism and human problems). I have written the last chapters in this book and they are about the above mentioned subjects.

One must always remember, however, that the way to learn is truly by opening the supreme book of life itself so that it can teach its mysteries to us.

Chapter 28.
THE JOB CALLED LIFE

Officially this book ended in the previous chapter in which we said our goodbyes, the reader and I. There is however, still something that is bothering me and stuck in the channels through which thoughts flow. These thoughts are in the system that my spiritual friend called the "conductor". They have not yet reached the "expresser". I have decided to study it a little closer and share it with you even after we have already said our goodbyes.

Here it is:

There is no doubt that the readers who are familiar with the concepts of spiritual reality covered in this book feel comfortable with the ideas I have exposed and the concepts I have dealt with. What happens is that a book is an object that circulates everywhere and carries its message, which is sometimes potentially disturbing and might cause "disorganization" in our personal microcosm. Our ideas are organized in such a way we are accustomed to. We know perfectly well where we can find this or that or how to walk through the halls and rooms of our mind in the same way a person who after living many years in the same house is able to find a book on a certain shelf in the dark because everything is familiar to him.

Suddenly someone comes into our house, changes the furniture and the rooms around, moving the bedroom furniture into the dining room and the library into the kitchen, or the couch to the backyard.

How can we organize this chaotic situation?

It is fair, then, to consider the case of those intelligent readers who are open to new ideas and proposals but who hadn't yet considered the possibility of such things being true, or, at least, hadn't considered this a vital element in the organization of our lives and in the way we care for the children in our life – our children, grandchildren, nieces and nephews or just friends' children.

So is it really true that we are all preexisting beings? Does this mean we have lived before and might even have met our parents,

CHAPTER 28.

siblings and friends in other existences? Does it mean that death is not this definitive and inevitable thing we thought it was? Am I in the wrong religion and should I change my philosophy of life?

Let's take it one step at a time.

If your internal life value evaluation system is truly outdated in relation to the basic concepts we covered in the book, it's true you need a good structural reinvention. This is not an urgent matter although I believe it is an important priority you should address. You won't be the first person or the only person or the last person who will suddenly find themselves facing a new reality they had not considered with due attention before. It doesn't matter. Let's move slowly.

It is probably a good idea to return to dr. Helen Wambach's precious book as she dealt with many people who went through the same perplexity.

I, myself, have witnessed the moment in which a person who was under hypnosis talked about the details of their previous life and was later awakened and heard their amazing testimonial. It was an educated man, a dentist who was intelligent and in good standing. He spoke about his previous life, something he had never thought about before. Besides how would he be able to conciliate this with his protestant beliefs and practices as he had been a catholic priest before?

I usually say that when we can't change the facts, something that happens quite often, we must change our stance towards them. As we know: When the mountain does not go to Mohamed, Mohamed goes to the mountain.

If the mountain doesn't come to us we must go to where *it* is, if we do really need to climb it. And we do!!!!

The subjects of Dr. Wambach's research are a group of different people who are either connected to different religious systems or are not interested in religion. Many of these people found themselves describing "impressions that conflicted with their conscious beliefs"

There was much surprise and perplexity.

I continued to believe that the information that reached my mind (said a subject) made no sense but its questions came about quickly and I remembered my answers. I was under the impression that if I had had more time I would have been able to answer them differently, because they conflicted with what I believe in.

This is a fact. If there is time to think, the conscious mind interferes and shapes the answers according to what the person thinks is right. It does not allow the subconscious mind, or the spiritual individuality, to express itself.

"Most of my patients, writes dr. Wambach, confessed that they were shocked at the information that emerged and that *they would need some time to digest all of that.* (my italics*)*

"I realized what a mystery I am to myself (says another lady) and I started thinking about the potential withheld in my forgotten past..."

As the reader might have noticed we are not dealing with vague and fleeting impressions but with unsuspected realities that touch the depths of our beings and carry a strong emotional power. I use to stress, in experiences like these, the importance of the emotion given rise to, and am happy dr. Wambach feels the same way about its importance. It is very hard, if not impossible, to fake such strong emotions. They are authentic as nobody is there to set up a farce or to play a role. Who would be fooled? Would they be fooling themselves? Besides, in quite a percentage of cases, the reality seen by a person, doesn't necessarily match what she (or he) *believes* to be true. Believing how things happen in such way or the other, is quite different from *observing* how they really happen.

This is why dr. Wambach tells us that "her patients were very silent and thoughtful once the regression session was over."

"They all had", she writes, "a distant look (…) and were obviously quiet and thoughtful (…)."

This is because they had just returned, as one of them stated, from a very long journey to an unknown place inside themselves."

***

I insist in saying in these final words, that I have no intention of proselytizing. I do not wish to convince you into joining the spiritist movement. I am not given to these merely statistical matters because, as I have mentioned before, spiritism does not consider itself the owner of the basic concepts its doctrinal structure is based on. The truth doesn't belong to one person; it belongs to everyone. It is

CHAPTER 28.

therefore your truth too, dear reader. The important thing in the task of managing the relationship between parents and children is the absolute certainty of the spiritual reality. That is to say, to know that we all carry within us a vast and little known universe that is extremely rich in potential. Realizing its existence may help us to better understand what I usually call *"the job of living"*

Another one of my favorite concepts is that we are only able to make progress by replacing obsolete and useless ideas by new ones which might at first seem traumatic to our personal system of thinking and living.

I also used to say that, besides God who is unchangeable, there is only one thing permanent in life: change. But one day I found out that Heraclitus had said the same thing so I lost the copyright to one of my favorite lines. After all, Heraclitus is also an intelligent man and the line still holds true. (Attention to the use of the present tense: He *is*, as he is alive like you and me.)

Deep inside we might miss some of the old and obsolete ideas which seemed comfortable and permanent but we end up liking the new arrangement better when we realize that more space is left for thinking and living. This will last until we need to replace old useless furniture by others and rearrange it in a more harmonic way once again. One day we are surprised with the reality of living in the much dreamed of Kingdom of God.

But after all, this is what life is all about: movement, maturity, realization, evolution unfolding towards infinity.

Dear reader, you know well by now that this is not a book. It is a conversation and conversations between friends have no end. Much has happened after I launched the first edition of this book in 1989. I would feel frustrated if I couldn't tell you that in 1991 I received a kind of "father diploma". I thought it would be my duty to share this joy with you. If you see a touch of pride in my tearful eyes what am I to do? After all nobody is perfect and there's a limit to human endurance!!!

Turn the page and check.

Chapter 29.
"FATHER DIPLOMA"

You have certainly seen one of those printed Mother Diplomas that you buy and have to fill out the blanks in the right places to give your mother, the special person who brought you into the world, on Mother's Day. I don't know if you've ever seen a Father Diploma. If you haven't you will see one now Please forgive my lack of modesty for showing it to you. I received it on the day my wife and I celebrated our forty ninth wedding anniversary. It was written by Ana-Maria, whom I talk about in the beginning of this book.

It is a dialog between the Eternal Father and I. The setting is heaven, in the year 1920.

St. Peter, the beloved Fisher of Souls who perpetually holds the keys to the kingdom of heaven, welcomes me and takes me to the Lord. I believe Ana-Maria was there, listening quietly behind a sheer cloud as she faithfully reproduced our conversation.

This is what she wrote:

"And how are you, my son?" He asked.

"Very well, Sir. And I am even better now in Your presence." I replied.

"It is wonderful that you think this way. But I called you here, you know, because you asked to go back and I decided you will go on the 5th."

"The fifth?"

"Yes. On earth they have things such as days, hours, months, etc. They follow the notion of time there."

"Oh, I see…"

"Well, your name will be Hermínio Corrêa de Miranda. Your mother Helena and your father Reduzindo are anxiously expecting for your arrival. You will be the first child of this couple who is very close to my Love."

CHAPTER 29.

"Yes Sir."

"Your life plan has already been decided according to your previous request. But, naturally, you will be free to decide to follow another plan, to change."

"Yes Sir."

"First you will be a son. Then you will be a godson, then a brother, then a student, and..."

"A student, my Lord?"

"Yes, a student, an uncle, a cousin, an employee and so on until you become a boyfriend, a fiancé and a husband and then a... FATHER. This is the most important category of all."

"FATHER, my Lord? I thought only You could be a Father."

"Oh you're right. Let's say that I am the FATHER of all fathers."

"Well, then..."

"But you will also be a father. You asked for three children; two girls and a boy."

"Wow, my Lord!"

"Yes. First there will be Inez, your lifelong partner, the mother of your children. Then Ana-Maria, Marta and Gilberto!"

"Ana-Maria, Marta and Gilberto?"

"Yes, this is what you asked for. They will cause a lot of trouble and will make you suffer but they will bring happiness which will make up for all of this. This is how parents think...."

"I see."

"Naturally this will only begin in 23 years."

"Ok, my Lord, when I am 23 years old."

"But, as I was saying, out of all the things you asked for, being a FATHER is the hardest thing to do on Earth. As the years go by it will be even harder."

"I understand, my Lord"...

"No son, you don't. But when the time comes you will know

what to do. Although there will be times of sacrifice, renunciation, agony and even revolt there will be a lot of understanding."

"My Lord, it seems very hard. There will be both revolt and understanding?"

"You're right. You should know. You asked for it."

"I'm scared, my Lord. To be a father, like You. I don't think I have what it takes."

"Who knows? Maybe in many years we will meet again and pick up where we left off…"

"Yes, my Lord…But I see two envelopes in your hands. Are they for me?"

"Ah, I was just getting there." Let's see. This one contains my instructions for your life as a father. Here are the solutions to all of the problems you will face with Ana-Maria, Marta and Gilberto. This is what you should tell them, what you should do, how you should advise them, what you should teach them, how you should reprimand them and you should also teach them how to follow their intuition. I will upload these instructions to your spirit's computer!"

"What's a computer my Lord?"

"One day you will know. When the time comes for you to solve a problem with one of your kids all you have to do is use your memory and all MY instructions will appear. Here is the program."

"Thank you my Lord but there must be a mistake, this is just a blank piece of paper!"

"No, my son, there is no mistake. What happens is that only fathers can read what is written there."

"Oh, I get it" What about the other envelope?"

"This one has just one word."

"Just one?"

"Yes, just one. And you will only be able to open this envelope on the day you feel the need to know something very important."

"Is that true, my Lord?"

"Yes."

CHAPTER 29.

"But what is it?' Is it something that has to do with my children?'

"Yes, I will explain." I know what you will think about your children. I know what they will think about you. But you won't know what they think of you as a father."

"Oh, well."

"So on the day you want to know what they think of you, go ahead and open this envelope. If at least one of them calls you what is written here on this sheet of paper you will have become even closer to ME as a FATHER."

"Yes, my Lord"

"Well the time has come. In a second you won't remember anything for many, many years. Go, Herminio. You have my blessing. Good luck!"

"Thank you Lord. I will miss you. I'll see you some day..."

The second act takes place on Earth in 1991. The couple is celebrating their 49th wedding anniversary. Ana-Maria gives me the following message:

"Dad, open that envelope today. Check and see if the word the Lord wrote wasn't...FRIEND.

"...it was."

***

So, this book that began with Ana-Maria ends with this page she created with the talent and the feeling she brought with her. She signed my "Father Diploma". It answers one of the questions I read in Ana-Maria's eyes when we met on this side of life. Remember? She asked "Will you be a good father to me?"

With my diploma I will be able to introduce myself *up there* as the worker Paulo talked about, who will not be ashamed of the work he performed here on Earth.

Chapter 30.
MY FATHER DIPLOMA PART 2: THE MISSION

I was invited by Alexandre Machado Rocha, my editor (Lachâtre) to sign my book at the "Bienal do Livro" (Book fair) in São Paulo, in May 2000 when a group of young couples approached us. They wanted to meet me in person, asked for autographs and handed me a beautiful dossier organized by people who knew something about computers and feelings. I knew nothing about the former as I still haven't made much progress in the area to this date. But I think I can say I know something about the latter as I have used feelings and emotions when writing. I believe a text without emotions and feelings is very cold, arid and even blurred. If my writing were distanced from my feelings it wouldn't reach the hearts of the people I write to. If a book lacks emotion it is because its author failed to add his own experiences, his need for solidarity and the wish to share the positive things he learned with his readers.

I had no idea that that night my emotions would take hold of me like they seldom had in all of my life.

This is one of the good things I plan to share with you, dear reader.

As you see, I added a new and unexpected chapter to this book which I called FATHER DIPLOMA, written by my daughter Ana Maria, my eldest daughter. Now I find myself needing to write a new chapter with one more magical but not less touching story.

The couples who came to me at the "Bienal" had one thing in common: they were all parents of Autistic children.

Unfortunately, we didn't have enough time to talk that night. Only when I got back to my hotel room was I able to take a look at the dossier they had prepared.

What I read triggered a flurry of emotions.

The cover of the dossier had these words at the top:

CHAPTER 30.

"Lachâtre Editors: We made our own cover for this great book."

The next page contained a copy of the cover of my book on Autism changing the title: "AUTISM: a spiritual reading" to "AUTISM: a fraternal reading".

Here is what came next.

***

There are many who enjoy movie sequels. I, for one, consider productions such as Rocky I, II, III, IV or Die Hard (and hard to watch) I,II,III to be questionable. But what I will show you here will have a strong impact on special people.

It is called: "Father Diploma-part 2: The Mission".

"Well, the time has come, Herminio. A second from now you will not remember any of this for many, many years. Go, Herminio. You have my blessing. Good Luck!" He said.

I replied: "Thank you my Lord. I shall miss you. I will see you when I come back"

"Wait son," he said. "I have one more envelope for you. It doesn't quite belong to you but it has to do with you."

"Does it concern my children, Lord?" I asked.

"In a way it does!" He said. "You may or may not commit to this envelope. It's up to you."

"But what's inside this envelope, my Lord?" I asked.

"My dear son, as I told you before, you will be a student, an uncle, a cousin, an employee, a boyfriend, a fiancé and a husband before you become a....Father. As I have also told you, you will have three children whom you will love a lot and will bring you lots of happiness. But Herminio, this envelope contains countless little envelopes. I don't how many, I haven't counted."

"Are there tiny envelopes inside the envelope?" I asked.

"Yes." He replied. These little envelopes are the children of other fathers and mothers. These little envelopes will reach them, unopened and will contain a great, sweet mystery. These envelopes/children are My Messages to these parents and to whoever is around them. Whoever opens these mini-envelopes using lots of love, my son, will be able to understand many important things."

"May I ask what things, my Lord?"

"One of the things they will learn is what a human being is in all its dimensions. Your mission, Herminio, will be to help these parents open these tiny envelopes." He said.

"I'm not quite sure I understand. It seems like a great responsibility. How can I help children who aren't my own? I don't even know if I will be a good father! How will I be able to help other parents?" I asked.

"You will know when and how, Herminio. Many will be doing the same trying to open these envelopes but you will do your share. Do you accept the mission? He asked.

"My lord" I replied. You have given me much strength, love and motivation. I am sure that I will always be able to count on you when times are hard. This is why I do accept my mission."

"I won't keep you any longer, my son. Go, Herminio. You have my blessing. Good luck. In a second you won't remember anything for many, many years."

"Thank you Lord, for your trust in me." I'll see you soon. I will miss You a lot!"

(The second act takes place on Earth in the year 2000. Herminio is signing one of his best known books at the 16th Bienal Internacional do Livro(International Book Fair), in São Paulo. He receives some papers. He recognizes them!!!! They are some of those little envelopes God had told him about. They are no longer closed. They are open and he realizes that there are many messages from God inside them. Herminio smiles and thanks God, his Lord and our Lord, for having trusted him with such a special mission...)

***

The following text, filled with love and emotion, was written by Cristina Aparecida H. Lopes, who speaks on behalf of herself and of her much beloved son Gabriel. Attached to the text was the following letter.

***

CHAPTER 30.

Dear Mr. Herminio.

Here are some of the little envelopes from God.

We, the parents, are making an effort to deserve these wonderful gifts our Creator has sent us and to understand and multiply His message. We wish to thank God who is so fair and infinitely good for sending us these little envelopes.

On November 10, 1998 I was very happy to receive a phone call from you thanking me for the e-mail I had sent to Lachâtre with comments about the book "Autism: a spiritual reading". It was a very strong moment for me emotionally.

I am the mother of Gabriel who is now 6 years old. He is doing extremely well. We live in Sorocaba, São Paulo. Gabi goes to a regular school and we have made much progress although he still can't walk.

In the discussion forum on the internet called Esauluz parents and professionals have exchanged ideas and feelings about the child who "is special in this life" under the light of the Spiritist Doctrine. We have chosen to follow it because as you say it is impossible to get to the bottom of anything if we don't allow spirituality into our lives. Isn't it true? You will note that Nilton Salvador, the author of "Vida de autista" (Life with Autism) is a member of this forum and will send you a message.[2]

> As of April 16, 2000 we have been systematically studying your book "Autism: a spiritual reading". Daniel, one of the list members writes a summary of each chapter and includes his observations. Afterwards, other participants are free to comment on it. So, when we found out you would be at the Bienal we decided to honor you trying to return some of the love you give to us through your books. (Gabriel's speech therapist is not a spiritist and she loves the book "Autism: a spiritual reading")

Mr. Miranda, I believe we form a fan-club. We still haven't read all of your books but we would surely love to!!!

I am sending you a big hug, a picture of Gabriel (we have three

---

[2] Nilton Salvador is a professional journalist and writer and has a son with Autism about whom he has written the book mentioned in this letter.

Gabriels on our list) and an excerpt from the book "O Castelo das aves Feridas" (The castle of wounded birds), whose author Nancy Puhlmann di Girolamo recommended me the book "Alquimia da Mente" (Alchemy of the mind):

"We are interdependent, interconnected. Some play the role of parents down there. Others are technicians and researchers. Some had their wings cut before and continue to have bonds of affection. Others were responsible for the cuts. Many are helping so that they don't have to lose their own wings...we are all like in the same family."

Thank you very much,

São Paulo, May 7, 2000

Cristina Aparecida H. Lopes and Gabriel

***

Claudia and Sidney R. A. Pereira wrote to me from Volta Redonda, Rio de Janeiro, my birthplace. They also received an envelope from God and were able to open it and find the message their Gabriel wanted to send me. Please see how beautiful it is.

***

Dear Mr. Herminio Miranda,

My name is Gabriel and I am 11 years old. I am happily passing through this life here on Earth with Autism. Mr. Miranda, can I call you friend? My mother Claudia asked me to tell you (even though I speak only with my eyes) that thanks to your book "Our Children are Spirits" she was able to find out about the love-filled doctrine called Spiritism. And also thanks to your book "Autism" she accepts our reality much better and faces our mission with more love. My mother and I would like to thank you very much for the wonderful job you have been doing writing such exciting books. She has read almost all of them. My dear friend, even if we haven't met, please know that you have made a big difference in our lives and have a very special place in our hearts.

Please receive our love and that of Esauluz! May God be with you!!!

Gabriel – Volta Redonda-Rio de Janeiro

***

CHAPTER 30.

Please read the beautiful testimonial sent to me by Silvânia Mendonça, the mother of André Luiz Rian who was 10 years old at the time in May, 2000.

***

My dear brother in Christ Herminio Miranda,

We are members of Esauluz. Esauluz is a discussion forum in the Internet that deals with the autistic child, or better said, of the child that *is* special (at the moment).

We are united in our children, in our strong need of learning the Law of Cause and Effect. United we stand in the same cause of love. Our children *are special* in "this life". We share our experiences, our messages, our dialogs, our lives under the light of the the Spiritist doctrine. What is most interesting is that there is no distance between us. We are in São Paulo, Rio de Janeiro, Fortaleza and in many other places including Portugal. We can feel the energy of this group at all times.

The name Esauluz comes from: "Espiritismo" (Spiritism), "Autismo"(Autism) and "Luz" (light/knowledge. Our purpose is simple: "Do learn, this is the law".

Please know, dear friend, that you were one of the people who inspired us when you wrote the following words in your book, "*Autism – a spiritual reading*": "If you can't cure the autistic child, love it. There is an important reason this child is near you. It will certainly be for his and your benefit....*Trust, work and wait.*"

This is what we are doing. We would like to publish our book with our ideas and we intend to dedicate as much love as we can to these children with special needs.

If you wish to learn a little more about our work at ESAULUZ, please speak to our dear friend and fellow forum member Nilton Salvador. You will also be able to learn more by e-mailing our coordinator, Eugenia, through the e-mail: esauluz@grupos.com. We are at your disposal. We admire your words and your work of love.

We kiss your heart tenderly. May Christ be with you.

Silvânia Mendonça, Representative of Esauluz in Belo Horizonte, Minas Gerais

Mother of André Luis Rian-10 years old, autistic

Here is Nilton Salvador's letter:

My dear Brother in this Journey Hermínio C. Miranda,

LIGHT AND PEACE!

Life didn't want us to meet this time but I am sure we will meet in the future because it is certainly true that nothing happens by chance.

These mothers and sisters in the selfless battle against Autism have chosen to write you this message as a token of their love for you who have inspired us so much especially after your book "Autism: a spiritual reading". Your book has soothingly helped us continue our saga with a greater understanding of what Divine Providence has wished for us.

Thanks to your wise and compassionate words we are able to become aware of how we should practice solidarity and love towards those around us who suffer from Autism and how this love regenerates us. Please receive, on their behalf and in my name our thanks through these words I write you. You and your work are much appreciated!!!

Light and Peace!

Nilton Salvador and family

Curitiba, Paraná

***

This letter was written by Arlete:

***

Dear Hermínio,

My name is Arlete.

I live in Fortaleza, in the state of Ceará. I am the mother of Thiago, 8 years old who has Down Syndrome and Autism (see attached photo)

In my quest to understand some existential questions and my son's condition more specifically I have become more acquainted with the Doctrine of Spiritism.

CHAPTER 30.

This contact has made a big difference in my life. A new world opens up to me with new values, new paths and new friends I have had the pleasure of being with, some on the internet, with whom I have shared fruitful experiences.

I felt very close to you while studying *"Autism: a spiritual reading"*. I was impressed by the clear and profound manner you deal with such a controversial and difficult subject. I am reading the book very slowly trying to follow you the closer I can. There is a lot to understand. I feel there is much to be learned...that there is a long way ahead of me.

I would like to congratulate you for the research you made and for giving us a scientific approach on Autism under the light of Spiritism.

Here in Fortaleza, we work at the Fundação Projeto Diferente Different Project Foundation), a non-profitable organization that cares for people with Autism. It is managed by the parents of the children and young people who are assisted in the Foundation. We work with difficulty to make this institution a reality and are very strong and determined.

Please pray for our work, for our children and for all of those who work in favor of those with special needs.

May God be with you always,

Arlete

***

These are the kind words written by Lie, Ivan and Gabi in an email dated May 17, 2000, soon after our meeting at the "Bienal":

***

Mr. Herminio,

How can I express in few words how happy I was to meet you. It was wonderful to give you a friendly hug and to thank you for your dedication to your fellow human beings.

You know, I owe you an explanation. I know you answer many questions people ask you. I am Lie, the mother of Gabriel Gustavo, who is special. He suffers from Autism. With his own light and strength, he has slowly been discovering new things in our world.

We are very grateful for such wonderful books such as *"Autism: a spiritual reading"*, *"Our children are spirits"*, among others. Your books are like a balm which soothes the soul.

Please forgive me for having taken so long to write to you. We are very simple people with simple habits. There is so much to learn and so much to share that sometimes loneliness haunts us but we won't give up.

One day, Mr. Herminio, I told my son: "I will never give up on you because I love you more than anything."

As you, yourself, said in your book: if you cannot cure the autistic child, love it." How can I not love someone who already existed within me long before I existed?

Dear brother Herminio, I wish you all the light in the world.

With eternal kindness,

Lie, Ivan and Gabi

***

This is my reply to all these wonderful words of love and kindness:

***

If I had received the Nobel Prize I would not be happier than I was when I read the exciting words you sent me. It was impossible for me to have a long conversation with those representatives of the group who came to see me at the Bienal. I was also unable to dedicate some time to my dear Autistic siblings who were there too.

I was only able to read the dossier you gave me when I was back at my hotel room that night. You lit up my heart. After reading your words I went to the bathroom to wash my face and in the mirror I saw an old man with tears on his face looking back at me feeling very moved. They were tears of joy, of thankfulness, of pure and fraternal love such as St. Peter would describe it: *"love that would cover a multitude of sins"*. It did cover many of mine.

I am very grateful to God, to Christ and to the devoted spiritual friends for having made it possible for me to write the book on Autism and to have written it with the emotional charge you found in it. I am equally grateful to you for having opened such a big space in

CHAPTER 30.

your hearts for this old man who now writes to you. I am very happy to know that the message I tried to convey was received by you and contributed to inspiring the wonderful work you are doing for yourselves and for these very special beings that were entrusted to you by the infinitely wise and merciful Holy Father.

I loved the expression: "children who are special in this life". I myself say that I am not always Hermínio, but that right now I am Hermínio. One day we will look back and realize this was a very special moment in our spiritual path. I am sure that in the future we will all be united in happiness and thankfulness. We will cry tears of joy, enough tears to wash the universe.

I send you all my love and respect and to those special people who are special due to some important reason. They are wonderful, sensitive, intelligent beings who have lived and suffered a great deal. They have enormous potential and need your support to help them study and learn from old lessons, rekindle their souls and go on living and growing spiritually in the direction of light. We came from the light and we live in the light although we do not always see it. Once an entity told me that she was surprised to know she was surrounded by light and hadn't noticed it earlier because she had been in the dark.

Jesus said: "The kingdom of God is within us". All we have to do is realize this so that He can project Himself around us. We are one family and wherever we go we go with God.

Thank you for existing and for having accepted me in your generous hearts. I will be following the wonderful work you have been doing as closely as possible.

God bless us all. Fraternally,

Herminio C. Miranda

PS1: I have the old habit of praying daily at 6:00 pm. I don't follow any rituals, texts, memorized formulas or special ceremonies. I just keep quiet inside and meditate, pray and speak to God, to Jesus, to the spiritual friends and, after all, to myself, in a relaxed manner. It is a moment of a close and intimate reverence and reunion with the superior beings who guide our steps. If and when you can, "come" in spirit and join me in this magic moment, if possible bringing along our dear ones who *are special (at the moment)*. Take their hands and speak to the Lord, thanking Him for the opportunity you have been given of being in their company and of knowing the tasks you must perform.

PS2: Another suggestion: something you - mom and dad - can do which has brought much happiness, is to be present at the moment your dear son or daughter is getting ready to sleep. At this time of quiet, peace and low lights when the child is just about to fall asleep speak softly in a calm and paused manner without startling the child. The child will be there listening to you, knowing that we are all surviving, immortal, reincarnate, perfectible entities.

Tell them how much you love them with all your heart and how grateful you are to God for having sent this special person to your life. Tell them you understand the temporary difficulties but that they can count on you for anything they might need: your love, support, presence and understanding. God has put them near us so that we can we can do very important work for the future of all.

Do not hesitate to tell them about reincarnation and the responsibility each one has towards the supreme gift of life. Although the person might apparently not realize what is going on, the spiritual being will know exactly what you are talking about.

God does not punish or cause suffering. The law does not punish, it is educational. Pain is a result of our conflicts with the cosmic order but the Lord's mercifulness is always at our disposal and an arm and a prayer away. We are all learning to make less and less mistakes. One day, we will be so close to perfection that there won't be any space for mistakes. It's up to us. We all have the right to happiness, peace and harmony. Ask your loved one to help you in the common project to build this future.

Once again I say goodbye fraternally.

HCM, the crying old man in the mirror

Rio, May 9, 2000

***

On May 23, 2000 I received a beautiful message from Claudia, Gabriel's mother:

***

CHAPTER 30.

Dear Mr. Herminio,

Please forgive me for bothering you again. After I reread your beautiful letter to Esauluz for the thousandth time I could not stop myself from writing this simple poem. Please know I'm not a poet. It was just my heart that wished to speak.

Please accept this humble and truthful gift.

May God be with you,

Claudia (mother of Gabriel, 11 years old)

***

To Herminio de Miranda

Love Song to the Old Man

> *In the mirror cries the Old Man*
>
> *His emotions catch him off guard, tears roll down his face.*
>
> *He feels weak. He cannot move, like a true spiritual child,*
>
> *He is moved by the importance of this moment and of an answer from God.*
>
> *Behind the mirror there is a Mother,*
>
> *Who is touched by the Old Man's fragility.*
>
> *Who wanted to be there to dry his tears.*
>
> *Little does the old man know how much he has done for the Mother...*
>
> *She would like to hug him and bring comfort to him.*
>
> *He was the one who taught the mother, in his writing*
>
> *About the beauty, the comfort and the wisdom of his Doctrine.*
>
> *He was also the one who taught her to forget the offenses she had suffered*
>
> *And to realize that we are all evolving spirits,*

And that we must receive love in order to forgive at the right time.

He taught her to be patient and to wait for the time to be forgiven.

Ah...old man in the mirror, do not cry.

A lot has happened and you cannot have everything.

But you have done so much through your work.

As a simple writer, as you call yourself, in your simplicity.

The mother is delighted with this simplicity.

She has drunken in the fountain of your wisdom,

Has grown flowers with your loving advice.

Her son's disease is no longer a disease. It is a blessing.

And it is with your words, Old man, that she slowly cures her child.

The mother has extended this loving process of cure until it is done completely.

Without haste, without fear, without miracles.

For she knows the cure will happen with her child's progress in a natural way. His progress never ends, you said.

And you old man, have made her cry less because of the hope you have given her.

In the words of your letter she has read more than a thousand times and has printed in her heart.

Today she smiles with your letter in her hand...

Put your head up, old friend and do not cry,

Do not suffer any longer.

You have brought light to so many voiceless children and tired parents.

You have been a gift, a blessing and have brought

CHAPTER 30.

comfort to so many.

The mother looks at you from behind the mirror again.

She asks Mary (the greatest of all Mothers) to watch over you.

To guide you by the hand,

To take you away from the mirror and make you travel in the feelings of

Each heart you have helped.

So that the Mother might again see you smile,

A child, again...

Claudia M. Pereira, May 20, 2000

***

Silvania Mendonça Almeida writes me these kind words. This is how she tells her story and especially that of André Luis Rian's in an email dated May 11, 2000.

***

Herminio, my dear friend and brother on this journey,

Allow me to call you this way. Permit my writing and invading your privacy. Forgive me but I could not let such a precious opportunity go by. My name is Silvânia Mendonça Almeida Margarida. I am the mother of André Luís Rian Mendonça Motta, who is ten years old and suffers from autism. I live in Belo Horizonte, I am a spiritist and as a result of much effort and study, a university teacher preparing for my doctorate in the Universidade Federal de Minas Gerais (Federal University of Minas Gerais).

My dear friend, let me tell you the story of my Andri Lums, as my dear friend Nilton Salvador calls him. Here it is. I wrote this a year ago in a forum on autism. André Luiz was 9 years old (he is now 10).

A perfect child. Perfect looks. A healthy, beautiful and happy child. In his way of course.

When he was 10-months- old he started crawling always smiling happily. When he was 10 months and 10 days old he stopped crawling and sat facing a corner. I waited for a month. His eyes stared fixedly at something. He started playing with the same toy car and making circular movements. He wouldn't play with any other toy car. I remember that I waited for a month and told my mother: "Mom, the baby stopped crawling. He only crawled for 10 days. What do you think is going on?"

"Nothing, dear." She answered. "Baby boys are lazier than baby girls."

So, when I noticed nothing was happening I decided to take him to an orthopedist to have him checked; something a mother would do.

The doctor ordered many tests and they couldn't find anything wrong with him. I decided to go see his pediatrician. Everything was well. I went to an endocrinologist. There was nothing wrong with his metabolism. I asked to see a pediatric neurologist who ordered a Fragile X test, a brain scan and an EEG. All tests came back normal.

What was wrong with André, I asked myself? What could it be? Would it be a good idea to see a psychiatrist? I went to see one just to be safe.

They ran all sorts of tests including tests done in the famous Dr. Sergio Danilo Pena's office. He is a world famous geneticist. They couldn't find anything wrong.

A second neurologist told me André Luis had cortical blindness. But how could he be blind if he seemed to understand what was going on on television?

I gave up this doctor and his diagnosis.

Why should he be taking medicine if the epilepsy diagnosis hadn't been confirmed?

I took him to a new neurologist who prescribed Clonazepam, Gamibetal and other medication.

From that day on I decided to give up diagnosis and prognosis. I would attack what seemed to be wrong. What was wrong in my point of view? The way he was always staring at a fixed point, the fact he didn't walk and talk. The fact he didn't react. Was it Autism?

Following doctor's orders and with my husband's approval I hired a physiotherapist.

CHAPTER 30.

They used the Bobath therapy on him. At first I could hear his screams from a distance. The maid became my enemy and left my house saying that I was heartless mother and that she would report me to the police. After some time, André started crawling. Finally at 2 years and a couple of months he started walking.

When I put up an ad to hire a physiotherapist for him 15 candidates showed up. All of them talked about MONEY but my son is not merchandise. I interviewed each one of them and didn't make any promises. There was only one girl fresh out of college who didn't mention anything about money. I hired her for the market price. André Luis started walking and becoming independent. His vestibular control, fine motor coordination and speech still needed work.

I didn't know André's true mental age.

We hired a speech therapist and an occupational therapist. We never gave up.

I started working all night long as if I had always known about autism. Although Andre did not have the diagnosis for autism, many people in the family "labeled" him so.

Night after night, day after day as I do to this day. Would Silvania and autism match?

How did I know my son was autistic? I didn't know but *I knew*. It's hard to explain.

Autism was there and I had to defeat it. I had been told the autistic child was not affectionate and didn't look at other people in the eye. This was not true of André.

Well, if I am wrong or right it will be up to God to decide. I'm not sorry for anything I've done.

Midnight, 1 AM, 2 AM and there I was.

I would say: "Dedé, wave bye bye at mommy." Never any answer.

I started crying, smiling, and fighting. No response.

I started threatening him in a good way. "Wave me bye-bye or I will take away your pacifier!" And I took away his pacifier. He would scream and move his arms around, he wanted the pacifier. It was three in the morning when I had finally gotten him to wave at me. Then I would go to sleep and start over at 6:00 am.

I would take away some of his favorite things such as toys or pillows. Authority and limits are part of my personality. I succeeded. I had entered André's world.

It was not only my authority, respect or fear on his part for I don't think he would have reacted so well if such were the case.

I discovered music, classical music, Roberto Carlos, Elvis Presley, the "Jovem Guarda"

I discovered stereotyping. I would sit down in front of him and mimic gestures he would make. In this way we communicated. I started telling him about this side of the world. About smiling, kindness, love, feelings. I showed him his sisters. I taught them (his sisters Carolina and Camilla) to love him when I was away. I taught them how to be mini-therapists. My husband followed the process. Everything was an excuse to learn. The window and the sky. Blue and the sky. I started getting through to André. The results started showing. André was starting to smile at the world.

So many times I pinched myself and pretended to cry.

At the same time I would pinch his little leg, his arm, twist his nose with no remorse. I would dress as a clown. I would jump, shout, jump, shout. I made crazy faces. I showed him a lot of physical affection and dared to say: "There is no such thing as autism. It doesn't exist! Who said it does?"

It is well to look for the other side without questioning yourself. Negative feelings, revolt, punishment and the feeling of guilt don't agree with cure.

I follow the proverb: "What can't be cured must be endured". Not in the sense of being afraid but meaning firmness of character and acceptance to face what is ahead of you. My child needs me to be strict in order to get well. The more he learns the more he will be closer to a cure.

People question me all the time: "Is something wrong with André's mind?" "Is he autistic?" I answer: "I don't know!"

Why should he be discriminated?

CHAPTER 30.

I answer: "André is special, very special." Then I joke: you know, if you studied anthropology as I do, you would know André is so special that he is an example of the new human race which will communicate via telepathy. I have nothing against autism: he is my life. But it is not like me to look for a label, an explanation which is so important for my family.

There is a lot of controversy surrounding André's case. When he was four I found out he could read. I told my husband and we started asking him to read words in the papers, magazines and television...It was true. André Luís could read. I can't explain how. And what about the meaning behind the words? Yes his cognitive mind was advanced enough for that. Later a psychologist who has been seeing him for five years confirmed everything. He has a fantastic visual memory.

In a recent interview at a private and expensive school in Belo Horizonte I said André could read. I am sure they didn't believe me. In the tests he was given he didn't read to them. They called me in. I bought him some candy (something wrong I did, buying his reading but it was the only way I could get him to read on such short notice) and went to the test.

At every candy André showed everything he had to show. I remember their jaws dropped and one of the teachers said his reading was "accidental" Honestly, I don't know what this means. How can he read? He can't speak.

André is currently enrolled in a public school in the Serra neighborhood, in Belo Horizonte. Six months after he started school they found out André could read without saying anything. They do special work with him because his classmates can't read (they will though, with God's help)

André who is now nine years old attends a psychologist twice a week, a speech therapist twice a week, a religious class on Saturdays. He goes to a special school with lots of special classes: music, social education, physical therapy, drama. Besides he has lots of classes with his mom.

I never leave him alone not even in the middle of the night, as always. But now there is one difference. I no longer have to use intimidation to get him to wave goodbye to me. He gives me one, two, three kisses. If I ask him he says "Tal" (Tchau: bye in Portuguese) or bye! The next morning he replies to my: hi, how are you? and when we pray together he says "Amen" at the end and "Our Lord".

I always talk to him and say: "André, you are very special to me. You are a handsome and intelligent boy. I love you so much. We will still laugh about all this one day. I don't know when and where but we will. Remember André, you are perfect. Don't forget your friends, love them very much."

There are many different songs we sing together. The discovery of who he is, the gestures, everything is important.

I would have still a lot to say but I will end here wishing much, much success to all parents of autistic children and the professionals who deal with this mysterious behavior.

Where I will end I do not know. What I do know is that I would do it all again and I wouldn't like it to be any different. I love my son, I love special children and I will fight for them to the end of this funny life of mine. Autism is a great challenge but loving thy neighbor and not rejecting him is a much bigger challenge.

Thank you for listening to me. May God be with you my friend on this journey.

Yours truly,

Silvania

***

Reflections of an old scribler:

I have something to add to these accounts. As one can see, they were written with an openness of heart and soul, at no time do these people complain or whine or show any signs of discouragement. They are not "mad" at God for having "chosen" them among millions of fathers and mothers to receive those tiny, closed "envelopes"

On the contrary, if not happy, they are at least optimistic and aware of the responsibility bestowed upon them by the divine laws that guide our every step.

They are optimistic people, absolutely dedicated to the noble task of driving someone who is *momentarily* different, to a meeting with himself (her) and helping him (her) to reintegrate the spiritual group

CHAPTER 30.

where they belong. These people were chosen to work and learn in a collective project which includes family members, mental health professionals and those who study, work and travel with them.

The renowned psychologist and writer Bruno Bettelheim correctly calls it "rebuilding of the personality".

Unfortunately he is better known today (2008) for his theory on "refrigerator mothers" (mothers who are indifferent and even hostile) than for his many intuitive insights on a still uncharted territory.

In these accounts there is not one single example of a "refrigerator mother". On the contrary, they are extremely devoted and fight the good fight, as Paulo de Tarso would call it, to find answers in an extremely unchartered and enigmatic territory. They are loving and unrelenting mothers who are interested only in the final victory and not interested in taking by force the fortress. Dr. Bettelheim believed to be empty, as in the title he gave to one of his most famous books. First of all, it is not an unassailable fortress as he himself demonstrated. Second, the stronghold is never empty. There is someone there, someone good who has suffered and was marked by wounds not yet healed but that are in a clear process of cure. Real cure.

As I was writing this text I came across the words of a well-known and competent doctor who emphatically stated that autism is an incurable disorder.

With all due respect to these devoted professionals and specifically to this doctor I do not wish to identify, autism *is not incurable* if it is considered within the perspective and expectations of reincarnation.

It is very true that, considering the narrow perspective of one and only existence, there are rare, almost dramatic exceptions of radical cure of this painful syndrome. When writing the book about autism more than ten years ago, I heard of only one case of radical cure- that of Raun Khalil Kaufman- the autistic son of the young couple Suzi and Barry Neil Kaufman. It is possible to affirm this not only from the father's testimonial but also from the boy himself who was interviewed and talked articulately about autism and what he and all the wonderful team who worked with the Kaufman's had gone through.

Dr. Temple Grandin became a brilliant and successful

professional while still suffering from autism. As strange as it may seem, she worked with her own perceived autisms, as Dr. Oliver Sacks, an internationally renowned specialist declared.

It might be then that we cannot cure our loved ones who are special *now* but there is no doubt that they will be cured. They have come to an earthly life in families who not only accept them but love them unconditionally with courage and devotion and believe that everything will work out and that we are sorting out old human problems which were stuck in drawers or swept under the carpets of our past lives. There are many of them who also have come to cure us of spiritual sore spots we don't even suspect.

It is understandable to hear that autism is incurable. Many of us think that earthly science and pharmacology must come up with some medication or therapeutic program for every human disturbance.

Many haven't noticed that in God's pharmacy there is only one medicine for all the physical, mental and emotional diseases of creatures. I said ALL of them. This little medicine is too simple and that is why it is not taken seriously although it does cure everything. You will not see pompous labels, sophisticated packaging, contraindications, uses or risk factors on this bottle. The label simply states: LOVE. Take always when your heart asks you to. It knows just when. But, just pick up a bottle in the shelves of the divine pharmacy and give those in need a few drops of it. You will then discover that God has given you powers to make miracles come true.

Before ending this account, I must update some facts, as much as it is possible to update facts that are quickly changing in the search for a consensus or in the search for a thread like the one the young and beautiful Ariadne[3] freed her beloved Theseus from a labyrinth and from death.

The book *"Autism- a spiritual reading"* was written in the last

---

[3] For those who don't remember I will tell you a summarized version of the love story I found in Wikipedia: Ariadne, the daughter of Minos, king of Crete fell in love with Theseus when he volunteered to kill the Minotaur who lived in the labyrinth so cleverly designed by Dedalus that it would be impossible for whoever went in to escape it alive and would be devoured by the Minotaur. Ariadne who wished to help her beloved gave him a sword and a ball of thread (Ariadne's thread) so that he could find his way back. Theseus was successful and went back to his homeland with Ariadne although his love for her was not the same as hers for him.

decade of the twentieth century and first published in October, 1998 based on the specialized literature of the time as can be seen in its bibliography.

As I write these lines ten years have passed and a lot has happened and a lot is yet to happen when it comes to the studies and research on autism which is still the enigmatic labyrinth we cannot find our way out of. We lack Ariadne's thread of spiritual reality. Or better, we still need to accept the fundamental concepts that rule the mechanisms through which such life operates around us. The same way that material reality is ruled by a set of specific laws. Over 2,300 years ago Aristotle noticed this division when he identified the material part of the universe and that which is beyond the physical. He called this metaphysics, not in the sense in which it is today understood in less philosophically prepared circles, somewhat as a synonym for occultism but in its real content defined as such in the Aurelio dictionary:

1. Philos. Part of philosophy which is often confused with it. and in different perspectives, presents the following general characteristics or some of them: a set of rational knowledge based on logical reasoning rather than on empirical methods. A system of thought based on or involving such inquiry as to give us the key to real truth as opposite to what is apparently true. (Cf. ontology)

2. Hist. Philosophy. According to Aristotle (see aristotelism): the study of beings as beings, and speculation over the first principles and first causes of beings.

3. Subtlety or transcendence while speaking

As I have mentioned in other writings of mine there was in the seventies, the beginning of a movement which pointed towards the existence of a spiritual component in human beings. Some names belonging to this movement : Helen Wambach, Edith Fiore, Raymond Moody Jr., George Ritchie and many others around the world. I could not leave out Dr. Ian Stevenson who left irrefutable scientific evidence on reincarnation and Dr. Elisabeth Kübler-Ross who, like it or not, radically changed the face of death.

In the eighties other writers followed who were equally convincing. The dominating mass though, which is guided by materialism, stubbornly rejected any other new approach that would allow opening windows and would air out concepts and postures wishing to explore the spiritual territory of life.

The dominating dogmatism of the more conservative academic circles left no room to even consider the spiritual aspects of life. The only thing that changed was the end of the use of the obsolete term "occultism" which was replaced by a more modern expression. The ones who were interested in such things were considered *New Age*. In other words, somewhat eccentric people, to say the least, would be interested in such ideas. The sarcastic tone of such an observation continues to this day.

In my book "Autism: a spiritual reading" I am not afraid to be considered ridiculous or to be identified as one who believes in concepts which are said to be pre-scientific such as the existence, preexistence and survival of beings as well as reincarnation and communications between the living and the dead.

This reminds me once more of the story I have seen in different versions and plots which is always instructive. It is the story of the little boy who was looking for a lost coin at night, under a lamp post in the park. When a passerby who wished to help him asked him what he was doing, he answered that actually he had lost a coin somewhere else under the trees in the park, but how could he find it in the darkness?

With all due respect, there are many researchers looking for the missing information under the bright lights of sophisticated labs when the phenomenon called "paranormality" (another euphemism of escape) is right there, or in the background in the shadows of erudite ignorance and prejudice. Such walls must be torn down so that we can make way for the future to go on. We, along with the future…

Progress does not chose paths which have already been chosen, it opens new roads where there are none.

As far as I can see there is the beginning of a new breeze in the search for a spiritual component for the human being, especially within our dear and misunderstood autistic friends.

I can find this in two recent books written by William Stillman: *Autism and the God connection*[4] and *The Soul of Autism*[5] which is

---

[4] Sourcebooks, 2006, Naperville, Illinois

[5] New Page Books, 2008, Franklin, Lakes, NJ

CHAPTER 30.

even more advanced on the new path the writer is opening through the wilderness of prejudice.

The first book received a special mention from Dr. Larry Dossey, an old friend of mine who wrote *"Space, time and medicine"* in 1982 who greatly contributed to shedding some light on certain aspects of the speculations I made in my book *Alchemy of the Mind.*

Dr. Dossey almost seems to have read Léon Denis when talking about *Autism and the God Connection...*

This book challenges the simplistic explanations on autism. It goes beyond the neurological aspects. It deals with our nature, our origins and our destiny, ie, our connection with the Absolute or whatever name one may call it.

William Stillman, a writer and consultant specializing in autism, is he himself a part of the autism spectrum as he suffers from Asperger's syndrome. Besides (is this just a coincidence?) he has psychic powers, if not to say clearly mediunic capacities. As can be seen in the book's subtitle the writer intends to find a "redefinition" for autism. The book is considered the first attempt to find spiritual aspects in this complex and very mysterious syndrome. More than this instead of considering autism a stigma or a tragedy, Stillman believes the world needs autism in order to call attention to what goes on in the spiritual dimension of life.

In his opinion- and I fully agree- autistic people are not retarded half-wits as many still think but gifted beings endowed with an extreme sensitivity and well defined faculties and perceptions. According to Stillman (and I once more agree with him) it is very important to always presume autistic people possess an intellect such as in the case of the so called *idiot savant* and those who suffer from Down Syndrome. The fact that they are unable to express all of this potential is exclusively due to limitations of the biological mechanism (physical body) to which they are connected. In my opinion[6], it can be the result of a decision made before the process of reincarnation, by rejecting the idea of living in the flesh, as Dr. Helen Wambach supposed. It is also possible that the reincarnating entity wishes to reduce the interference of consciousness and to prioritize a

---

[6] See "Autism: a spiritual reading" and "Alchemy of the Mind, both published by Lachâtre.

more noble activity, an intuitive, non-verbal activity of the right cerebral hemisphere to which individuality is connected, that is to say, the spirit itself. Meanwhile the soul (personality) is connected to the left hemisphere. Stillman's theory that autism points in the direction of a new era should therefore be considered worthy of thought and research.

In his book *Autism and the God connection*,(Sourcebooks, 2006, p. 25) Stillman says that around 1990- the period I dedicated myself to a deeper research on autism in order to write my book- statistics showed one case of autism for every 10.000 American children. From this moment on there was an amazing and unexplained increase in the incidence of cases.

In the first chapter of his book entitled *The world needs Autism* (page 33) in the book *The Soul of Autism(2008)* Stillman includes an observation made by Julie Krasnow, published in the Indianapolis Star in the beginning of 2007 which states:

"With one in 166 children being diagnosed with autism, it can no longer be called rare. We have an epidemic on our hands. Every 16 minutes, another child is diagnosed with autism." Julie Krasnow, Indianapolis Star

In the author"s survey published in Time Magazine on May 6, 2002 he found that one out of every 150 children suffering from some kind of disturbance suffered from afflictions related to the spectrum of autism.

I must add that in a recent "Oprah" show in mid 2008, dedicated to autism, one of the mothers being interviewed affirmed that she had checked and statistics showed one case out of 96 children!

Some say this is due, at least in great part, to a better understanding of the diagnosis on the part of the medical community who had been in the dark for so long. In the opinion of many specialists, however, this does not account for the significant increase in numbers. In other words, it is obvious that the possibility of a better diagnosis has contributed to a significant increase in identified cases as such but it is impossible not to consider that in this same period there was an amazing outbreak of cases, that even the qualitative factor of a correct diagnosis is, by itself, hard to justify or clarify.

The Time Magazine article estimated at the time an incidence of

CHAPTER 30.

425,000 cases of autism in the United States alone but this number is being changed to 500,000 as I am now writing, in August, 2008. The institution known as CDC – www.cdc.gov states that in 2003, fifty three children born daily in the US were diagnosed as suffering from afflictions belonging to the autism spectrum. This adds up to 19,000 a year.

There is definitely something new going on. What message that still hasn't been decoded would explain the dramatic worldwide increase in the number of cases of autism?

William Stillman is troubled by similar questions. He suggests speculative answers which are worthy of attention.

One of the author's correspondents says she considers autism a challenge rather than a failure.

She is right. Stillman receives many testimonials on his website[7] from mothers especially but also from fathers, grandparents, aunts and uncles and siblings of autistics.

The tone of these testimonials is always emotion and love, acceptance, fight and never despair or revolt. "…if Autism hadn't happened to our family-says a writer- I would never have learned so much!"

Autism has led many, many people to make dramatic changes within themselves and to others around them, beginning by the own autists in the family and in the environment in which they live. Here are some examples: "I have become more patient", says someone. "Or more humble". "Or less selfish." "I started caring about things I ignored or looked down on before." "I realized that the important thing in life is not the wild fight for personal success and for money."

Above all, however, there are many who have convinced themselves of an unsuspected spiritual reality they had never dreamed of. Or of an entirely different point of view they had regarding this subject. Autistics are not half-wits who are unable to understand what goes on around them. They are capable of thinking and feeling and therefore loving and understanding that they are loved. The difficulty they face is not in understanding life but in expressing, let us say, in "our language" what they think and feel.

---

[7] www.williamstillman.com

This is why Stillman planted his flag on a basic premise: one must always presume that the autist possesses an active intellectual capacity which is usually above-average, sensitive, creative and well-informed. Moreover, it is important to state that many of them possess explicitly mediunic faculties. Stillman mentions (page 225-226)"The soul of autism" the following themes which seem to be present in the experiences of autistics: a previous existence (life before life), premonitions, telepathy, communication with animals, connections with entities who have passed away (usually a grandmother or grandfather),visions of discarnate spirits, wayward spirits (those who roam about as used in Kardec's writings) and ghosts, communication with ethereal, kind creatures who are called angels[8] by some. And consequently, I might add reincarnation and communication between the "living" and the "dead".

The author has, therefore, good reasons to believe that the alarming growth in the number of cases of autism is bringing about an unexpected interest in the spiritual aspects of life, which he considers to be the dawning of a "new humanity" (The Soul of Autism, p.55)

I have some personal ideas to add to the debate. In order to exhibit them using satisfactory evidence I would need more space than I have here. Anyway I will add some short observations.

In my opinion, Stillman refers - although not with the same words- to a great number of pioneers, showing us the possibility of using the right side of the brain instead of the predominantly used left side. The left side is verbal, analytical and enables us to do the small things we do every day. One's personality manifests itself on this left side and is closely connected to the right, non verbal, intuitive, unconscious right side where all of one's personal files relating to past lives are stored.[9]

---

[8] There is a lot of literature around regarding this subject in many languages. A lot might be considered fantasy. The term angel comes from the greek ângellos which simply means "messenger" and not necessarily a being endowed with benevolence as theology would have it. The verb, by the way, is translated into Portuguese as: to announce, to make known, to publish, to inform, to warn. This definition can be found in the Greek-Portuguese dictionary written by Rudolf Bölting, published by Imprensa Nacional Editors, Rio, 1941.

[9] Readers who are more interested in this subject should look up my book "Alchemy of the Mind".

CHAPTER 30.

On the other hand Pietro Ubaldi writes in his A Grande Síntese (The Great Synthesis) that the said logical, analytical, rational process of men has already offered all it has to human progress. The next step, according to the entity who dictated the book to professor Ubaldi, is intuition, which works through synthesis, free from limitations of oral language and free from the step by step analysis.

Dr. Temple Grandin is a clear example of this bold hypothesis which can be seen in the evolutionary roads of the future. Grandin, a wonderful proclaimed autistic, works by using the right side of her brain. Her thought process is non-verbal and uses creative synthesis and images. She jumps to conclusions without using boring analytical steps.

She is the first to say she "thinks" by means of images and not words at the same time she is sorry that more was not invested on her linguistic capacity as those who cared for her were basically concerned about her inner self.

Even so she was able to develop her geniality using her autism and not denying it. With all naiveté, she admits she isn't able to understand what goes on between Romeo and Juliet and doesn't get jokes or irony but, on the other hand, she is able to think up an elaborate industrial project in her mind without using sophisticated computer programs or drawing boards. Her privileged mind which possesses an infallible memory knows where each part belongs down to the smallest screw. When the system is ready she is able to virtually test-run it looking for flaws. She uses the right side of the brain when doing this and if, by mistake, she resorts to the left side she gets confused.

How can we not presume in a person like this the presence of a brilliant mind behind autism just because the physical, psychological and emotional limitations don't allow her to express what her spirit is thinking the same way we"normal" people can?

The renowned Dr. Oliver Sacks became so impressed with her that he included her in his "7 paradoxical stories" which are part of his book "An anthropologist in Mars".

Many geniuses from the past and present have been said to have autistic characteristics without any demerit. Charles Darwin, Albert Einstein and Bill Gates are some examples. As for myself, I would not be surprised if some weirdness or eccentricities in geniuses as

Van Gogh, Beethoven, Dali, Mondriani and so many others, would have autistic components.

It is really no surprise that, according to Stillman, 71% of American readers are interested in books about autism.

It is also a fact that traditional religions have been under scrutiny or at least questioned, specialy when they lack in their concept the obvious evidence of reincarnation and communication between living and dead, to mention only two factors.

Besides there are many people who become shocked by the surprise of having a family member or a neighbor or friends with children diagnosed with autism and bring to new ideological and theological positions, residues of dogmas and teachings they are used to believing over the years. They are obsolete concepts such as hell, devils, angels and divine punishment, singleness of an earthly life and other inconsistencies and fantasies.

It is sad to realize the enormous absence of the simple, wise and intelligent doctrine of the spirits.

Finally, I patiently give you a word of consolation: One day we will all know we are spirits. Wherever we are in time and space, both infinite, we will know how God created the autistics and how he created us.

BIBLIOGRAPHY

ANJOS, LUCIANO DOS & MIRANDA, HERMINIO C. De Kennedy ao homem artificial. Rio, FEB, 1975.

AMORIM, DEOLINDO & MIRANDA, HERMINIO C. O espiritismo e os problemas humanos. São Paulo, USE, 1985

CAPRA, FRITJOF. O Tao da Física. São Paulo, Pensamento, 1986

LOBATO, MONTEIRO. A barca de Gleyre. São Paulo, Cia.Editora Nacional.

LOHER, FRANKLIN. The power of prayer on plants

MIRANDA, HERMINIO C. Diálogo com as sombras. Rio de Janeiro, FEB.

_____. O exilado. São Paulo, Correio Fraterno do ABC, 1985.

_____. Diversidade dos carismas. Lachâtre, Niteroi, 1993

_____. " Os oito filhos que eu não quis". Folha espírita. São Paulo, 1985

_____. A Memória e o Tempo. Lachâtre, Niteroi, 1994

SANTOS, JORGE ANDRÉA DOS. Os insondáveis caminhos da vida. Rio de Janeiro, Fon-Fon e Seleta, 1981

STEVENSON, IAN. Twenty cases suggestive of reincarnation. SPR,1966.

STLLMAN, WLLIAM, Autism and the God Connection, Source Books, Naperville, Illionois, 2006

STILLMAN, WILLIAM, The Soul of Autism, New Page Books, A Division of Carrer Press, Inc., Franklin Lakes, NJ., 2008

WAMBACH, HELEN. Life before life. New York, Bantam Books, 1979

WATSON, LYALL. Supernature. London, Coronet Books, 1974

_____. The Romeo error. New York, Dell Publishing Co., 1976

Made in the USA
Charleston, SC
06 April 2011